PRAISE FOR *TIMES O*

"A riveting story of living and overcoming . . . a particularly relevant story in light of the COVID-19 fears and losses that so many are feeling today, Gregg leads us through his decision making, and battles, his setbacks and leaps forward . . . a gritty and inspiring life story!"

—REAR ADMIRAL RICHARD W. SCHNEIDER
United States Coast Guard Reserve (retired), President Emeritus,
Norwich University, Northfield, Vermont

"*Times of Perseverance* is both challenging and compelling. Gregg's story will be encouraging to you as he details how he overcame trials through the power of Jesus. It is a great reminder to us all about the faithfulness of our God and how he uses life's circumstances to draw us closer to him."

—DAN PLOURDE
Lead Pastor, Calvary Church, Jupiter, Florida

"I love hearing testimonies of God's grace in the midst of life's pitiless hardships. You will likewise love God's dynamic provisions as he moves, seemingly silent at times but matter of fact, in the life of Gregg. God's hand is evident in the life of my friend and believing Jewish brother. I highly recommend this book, *Times of Perseverance: Hope and Healing on the Battlefields of Life*. You will find it inspiring as God works writing your own journey of grace."

—JAY A. FOSTER
Dean of Christian Counseling and Director of Prison Ministries,
Louisiana Baptist University and Seminary, Shreveport, Louisiana

"I have known Gregg for several years. His life has shaped his passion for people to know the sustaining power of Jesus as healer and giver of purpose, and most importantly, Savior. It is a fascinating journey that can be an inspiration to all that read it."

—CRAIG BARRACK
Youth Pastor, First Baptist Church Llano, Llano, Texas

"This book is a story of one man's journey to overcome great physical, mental, and emotional hardships. It is a story of inspiration and courage, and of faith in a God that heals. A story that can bring hope to anyone that is struggling and to help them find the strength and the faith in enduring and overcoming the tragedies that have become part of their lives."

—PATRICK B. SIMPSON
Professor of History, Cedar Valley College, Lancaster, Texas

Times of Perseverance

Times of Perseverance

Hope and Healing on the Battlefields of Life

GREGG L. GROSSMAN

foreword by Scott Gray

RESOURCE *Publications* · Eugene, Oregon

TIMES OF PERSEVERANCE
Hope and Healing on the Battlefields of Life

Resource Publications
An Imprint of Wipf and Stock Publishers
199 W. 8th Ave., Suite 3
Eugene, OR 97401

www.wipfandstock.com

PAPERBACK ISBN: 978-1-7252-7059-6
HARDCOVER ISBN: 978-1-7252-7060-2
EBOOK ISBN: 978-1-7252-7061-9

07/09/21

To my parents, I honor you both in the presence of *HaShem* (Exod 20:12).

For my precious wife and love of my life, Valerie Joy, your unconditional love and friendship have sustained and blessed our marriage. Your love has been patient and kind (see 1 Cor 13:4–7).

To all those who have been wounded in life, this book is for you.

Survivors never, ever quit!

"My grace is sufficient for you,
for My strength is made perfect in weakness."
—2 Corinthians 12:9

Contents

Foreword

I would like to share with you something that took place one particular Saturday morning a few years ago. The week leading up to it had been busy and it was a struggle for me to get out of bed. I had to get up because there was a men's ministry breakfast taking place at my church and I needed to be there. I thought to myself that morning, "Lord, why could this event not have happened next week?" I was tired and just did not feel like going. However, I needed to be there not only because I am the pastor but also because I needed to greet the guest speaker who had been invited to speak at our meeting. That was the day that I met Gregg Grossman. He was our guest speaker for the day. Not only did he bless us as we opened God's Word together, but I found out that he and I have more in common than I have time to write about here. We both once lived in Ft. Lauderdale, had been called into ministry, and had a love for the Hebrew Scriptures. We instantly became friends and me forcing myself out of bed that morning all of the sudden turned into much more of a reward than it was a chore.

I have since been fortunate enough to collaborate with Gregg in the ministry on several occasions. On one of those occasions, he came to our church and led our congregation in a Passover meal called "Christ in the Passover." During this event he helped our people to see how Jesus is present even in the most sacred events of the Old Testament.

One of the great opportunities that God gives to pastors is that of building relationships with others in ministry. While ministering to the needs of others, the pastor sometimes feels as if he is out alone on an island and there is no one to minister to him because very few can relate to his plight. When he is able to find encouragement from someone who shares a common love for the Word of God and passion for ministry, then he has found a great blessing. I have found such a blessing in Gregg Grossman.

I encourage you to read Gregg's book because it is a glimpse into the soul of the man that I have since gotten to know and his gratitude for what the Lord has done for him. There are two great passions in Gregg's life. First is his love for Jesus Christ and second is his love for the Jewish people. It is only natural that these two passions come together in the ministry that God has given him in reaching the Jewish people for the glory of Christ. This is not a ministry that he is just equipped for; it is one that he is built for. As you read his book, you will see that everything that Gregg has experienced in life has prepared him for this very thing.

This book is a very personal story of coming to faith in Jesus Christ. In it you will read about a journey that is guided by the providence of God every step of the way. The events that take place within these chapters are simply too coincidental to be coincidence. The only logical conclusion is that the sovereign hand of God was working in him in a very special way and preparing him for a very special ministry. You will notice this throughout the book, as you see that even before he became a Christian, Gregg was compelled to recognize the fact that there was no help for him outside of Christ.

The odds against him becoming an ambassador who heralds Jesus as king were overwhelming, a son born to Jewish parents and raised in a household where strict adherence to Reform Judaism was a way of life. He was taught to have faith in the *Torah* and his ability to keep it. Gregg would later learn that it was not the keeping of the Law that would make him stand clean before a holy God, nor was it the sacrificial system contained in the Hebrew Scriptures. The only sacrifice potent enough to cleanse him was that which was made by Jesus on the cross.

After submitting himself to Jesus, Gregg suffered a great degree of rejection from the family that he loved. In spite of all this, God chose to place his mighty hand upon him and use him as a mouthpiece trumpeting the grace of God, which is received only through the sacrifice of Jesus Christ.

Times of Perseverance: Hope and Healing on the Battlefields of Life is not just a plea for the Jewish people to recognize their need to see Jesus as the Christ. It is much more than that. It is a captivating story about the power of God and how it has worked in one man's life. I highly encourage you to immerse yourself into the pages that follow so that you can see for yourself what God has done in Gregg's life, and therefore be encouraged about what he might be doing in yours as well.

SCOTT GRAY, MA
Pastor, First Baptist Church of Mesquite
Mesquite, Texas

Preface

The year was 2011 and I informed my wife, Valerie, about a desire to write a book. Was this a capricious, grandiose moment of fantasy? Undeniably, for that moment in time exemplified a transparent yet genuine desire to portray the experiential landscape of life, namely, a true story that not only captured a pristine theological and psychological journey to God through Jesus Christ, but in essence became the catalyst for challenging the reader, while connecting with them to provide a voice of encouragement through life application. Don Haskins, my former singles pastor, once remarked, "The lessons of a lifetime aren't learned in a single moment." Individual pieces that encompass the intricate design of a puzzle tell a story, for each piece is much like the tapestry of human life. And when the gestalt of human phenomena, albeit theological, psychological, interpersonal, and religion, coalesce, the completed portrait not only tells a story, but in essence the individualized components do indeed speak volumes about the experiential nature of life. Hence, this story addresses three pivotal dilemmas of human existence. First, it reminds people of all ages that material items, education, human effort, and status, although noble in and of themselves within the world, never promise salvation, eternal life, or a relationship with God through Jesus Christ. Second, Christians and Jews would benefit from sitting down in a diplomatic manner to learn about each other's lives. When both parties lay aside theological differences and meet each other where they are, it is then and only then that they can truly listen and understand each other, while studying the Scriptures together. Finally, Christians must embrace the "lived experiences" of the Jewish people, notably their human strengths and human limitations, while supporting them to fulfill God's will for their lives.

This book encapsulates an autobiographical component while underscoring the need to accentuate the value of lived experience. Each of us possess a story to tell; a genuine yet perceptual account of the world through our own eyes, so to speak, that becomes manifested through the faculties of knowing and experience within the orbit of life. This book consummates my survival from a challenging adolescence and clearly emphasizes the experiential vestiges from young adulthood. God captivated my attention at a young age, and for that matter remained sublime below the periphery of conscious awareness.

This compelling narrative stands juxtaposed with the dramatic scope of a cinematic production. Yes, indeed, the character transformation of Gregg L. Grossman was converted from within that intrinsic yet peripheral plane of existence harboring along the epistemological coastline of life. Hence the search for God meant that an affluent Reform Jew raised in a New York City borough would eventually travel the full gamut, theologically speaking, thus revealing to the reader God's presence, while demonstrating the lifelong yet tenured process of sanctification. The reader will appreciate the transparent candor, glean from the application-oriented chapter epilogues, and will be challenged with the eternal truth from Scripture. Finally, it is my sincere prayer that the *Jehovah Shalom* (Heb., God of Peace) captures our attention, penetrates our hearts by the Holy Spirit, and connects with people to share the great news of salvation which is found in Jesus Christ (Heb., *Yeshua HaMashiach*).

GREGG L. GROSSMAN, PhD
Spring 2020

Acknowledgments

This book is dedicated to God and the Lord Jesus Christ. "He has delivered us from the power of darkness and conveyed *us* into the kingdom of the Son of His love, in whom we have redemption through His blood, the forgiveness of sins" (Col 1:13–14). I would like to thank the ministries who ministered to me through the mediums of radio and print. Their sermons were both inspiring and encouraging and I am grateful for their prayers before coming to the Lord in 1992. My pastors, both past and current, have believed in me and played a significant role with my persevering to succeed as a believer in Jesus Christ. Two godly men inspired and encouraged my early walk with the Lord. The first was Dan Plourde, lead pastor of Calvary Church, Jupiter, Florida. His encouragement and sound biblical principles shaped my character during the early years as a believer in Jesus Christ. Don Haskins, the senior pastor of Calvary Chapel Christian Fellowship in Sarasota, Florida, provided sound biblical wisdom over the years. I am blessed to know Dr. Charles L. Wilson, the senior pastor at Central Baptist Church in Crandall, Texas. His friendship, spiritual guidance, teaching, and prayers played a pivotal role in the development of this book. I am thankful for Donna Poirier, who never stopped believing in me.

My appreciation to my graduate professors at Trinity Theological Seminary, for they have dedicated their lives to the spiritual and learning condition of God's people. I am deeply grateful to them for believing in my academic potential to teach his people and serve God in the body of Christ. I salute the president of Trinity College of the Bible and Theological Seminary, Dr. Braxton Hunter, and Dr. Johnathan Pritchett, the vice president of academic affairs. I appreciate my two professors, Dr. Elbert E. Elliott and Dr. James Chatham. These four men epitomize godly servant leaders who are dedicated to training men and women to serve Jesus Christ in the twenty-first century. To the Wipf and Stock publishing team, thank you for allowing me to share my story with the world.

My brother, Todd, is my real hero, for he is a man who watched over and protected me while growing up. Finally, thanksgiving goes to God and my Lord Jesus Christ, who have preserved, sustained, and sanctified me for service. The psalmist states:

> Behold, God *is* my helper;
> The Lord *is* with those who uphold my life. (Ps 54:4)

Introduction

Within the middle-class foreground of a New York City borough resides this autobiographical narrative depicting a Jewish boy's spiritual journey to Christ. The hierarchical system of the synagogue, coupled with parental discord, reveals a precocious Jewish man's quest for the meaning of God. Furthermore, this Jewish young man's search for deity began with seeking God outside his apartment window, continued through young adulthood with a summer trip to Israel, and reached a turning point with failing grades in college. Although a door opened to finish college, the pinnacle of this story is the severe traumatic brain injury of his older brother, Todd, and the author's near-death experience of traumatic brain injury, which was healed by the Lord. This story captures a longitudinal yet panoramic review of the circumstances leading up to a Jewish man coming to faith in Jesus Christ. The book exemplifies four unique concepts. First, this Jewish young man's search for God demonstrates an inalienable yearning for the Creator. Second, this search reveals the presence of specific people that were divinely positioned by God in the author's life. Third, the spiritual rebirth of this wounded Jew invariably means that past and current mistakes in life were forgiven and that God through Jesus Christ was in control of his life. God healed and restored this Jewish man for service and used him to reconcile an estranged father-son relationship. Finally, this story provides lucid evidence from journal entries that the Lord leads a person to himself in times of grief, suffering, human error, and life adversity.

The brain-injured and their families will appreciate and relate to this experiential account of survival from personal and family traumatic brain injury, while receiving hope, encouragement, and inspiration with the life-long challenges that accompany neurological impairment. Second, this book will challenge believers' lives while stimulating their faith in Jesus Christ; if Christians are estranged from God, they will be guided back to him. Third, the Jewish people will have an opportunity to learn about the Messiah that they are still waiting for, and Messianic Jews will appreciate the value and sacredness of Jewish identity while living out their Jewishness with Christians in the body of Messiah. Finally, this book appeals to the secular humanist with a zeal for knowledge. For the secular soul who is committed to worldly ideas that are antithetical to Scripture discovers the limitations of human knowledge, while learning about Jesus Christ and his gift of eternal life. This genuine account of parental discord, human error, and scholarship may pierce the impenetrable heart of the atheist and the agnostic.

ENGAGING THE MAINSTREAM

The book appeals to a broad audience within the church and the general population, while remaining indispensable for Christians, unbelievers, and the injured of society who need the gospel of Jesus Christ. There is an urgent need for this book in churches, synagogues, Christian and secular universities, families, cities, general and rehabilitation hospitals, nursing homes, and finally the global sphere. Moreover, this book targets a broad segment of the population. For example, high school and college students learn that true life purpose is found in Jesus Christ. Millennials discover that job, peer, or societal expectations require them to be true to God, true to his Word, and true to his people. Single parents are inspired to rear their children in the Lord, and divorced people discover the true source of perseverance, while learning about forgiveness and familial restoration. Young and middle-aged professionals are challenged to redefine their interpretation of success, while contemplating life purpose. Retirees and senior adults recognize that they have life stories and that their time on the earth is coming to an end. They appreciate the spiritual value of receiving Jesus Christ as Savior in order to obtain eternal life. This story represents a timeless message for a wounded humanity that is coping with the deleterious consequences of the coronavirus. Finally, this book appeals to the physically, emotionally, and spiritually injured of society to reconsider their circumstances by seeking God and his Son through Scripture.

INTENTIONAL OBJECTIVES

God's healing and restoration is available to those who are saved. And for those who are unsaved, God leads them unconsciously to himself through confessing with their mouth Jesus Christ as Lord, and if they believe in their heart that Christ was raised from the dead, they will be saved (see Rom 10:9–10). The goal of this book is to glorify God through his Son, Jesus Christ, and to illustrate how God healed and restored me from serious head traumas through faith in his Word. I hope to share my faith, strength, inspiration, and hope to people who are saved or have not had the opportunity to hear the gospel. The purpose of this book is to demonstrate how God uses mistakes and accidents in our lives for his glory. I will share about my older brother, Todd, who had a car accident that resulted in a severe traumatic brain injury in 1988, and how his accident unconsciously led me to the Lord. There will be documented evidence from journals to prove that God leads a person to himself, especially in times of tragedy. Moreover, I hope to share my near-death experience of being struck by a moving automobile in 1992. This accident resulted in a severe concussion and serious injuries. Surviving and recovering from a family member's severe traumatic brain injury as well as my own traumatic brain injury was possible only with the assistance from faith, family, and friends. I will also talk about another auto accident which resulted in a mild traumatic brain injury on November 3, 2011. This auto accident, in which I failed to yield the right of way, resulted in a healing from God that inspired me to write a book about my personal and family members' experience with traumatic brain injury. Even if we make mistakes in our lives, God still loves us with a love that is incomprehensible to the human mind. If you are spiritually, emotionally, or physically injured, may this psalm of David comfort your weary soul:

> The *righteous* cry out, and the LORD hears,
> And delivers them out of all their troubles.
> The LORD *is* near to those who have a broken heart,
> And saves such as have a contrite spirit. (Ps 34:17–18)

1

Early Remembrances

Lifeworld of Judaism

"Look, I go forward, but He is not *there*,
And backward, but I cannot perceive Him;
When He works on the left hand, I cannot behold *Him*;
When He turns to the right hand, I cannot see *Him.*"
—JOB 23:8-9

I was raised as a Reform Jew in Queens, New York. My parents divorced when I was nine years old and Mom tried her best to instill the Jewish faith into my life. I recall being eleven years old and gazing out the window to see if I could see God. I looked at the world outside my apartment window and couldn't fathom who God was or who God is. The synagogue tried to teach me through Jewish liturgy and ceremonial traditions. Although God remained a profound enigma to me while growing up, I possessed a curiosity to know *Adonai* (Heb., Lord). At the age of eleven, in addition to weekly Sunday school, it was required by the synagogue to undertake intensive Hebrew lessons one day a week for two years. The synagogue was close to my home so I was able to walk there after school in preparation for the *bar mitzvah*. The aforementioned Hebrew word, *bar mitzvah*, literally means "son of the Commandment."[1] At thirteen years old, I was preparing to be called to the *Torah* during a Saturday morning Shabbat service. The word *Torah* in Hebrew is literally translated as "teaching,"[2] and comprises the Pentateuch, the five books of Moses: Genesis, Exodus, Leviticus, Numbers, and Deuteronomy. *The Shengold Jewish Encyclopedia* explains:

> Though originally *Torah* may have applied only to the Ten Commandments and later to the **Pentateuch,** it was from an early period employed as a general term to cover all Jewish law, including the vast mass of teachings recorded in the **Talmud** and other rabbinical works. This latter literature was called Oral Torah, or Tradition, as opposed to Written Torah, or Written Law.[3]

This is the bedroom where I gazed out of my apartment window and wondered who God was and is.

---

1. See Schreiber et al., eds., *Shengold Jewish Encyclopedia*, 43.
2. See Schreiber et al., eds., *Shengold Jewish Encyclopedia*, 262.
3. Schreiber et al., eds., *Shengold Jewish Encyclopedia*, 262.

The fun part of the *bar mitzvah* experience was receiving gifts from family and friends. The not-so-fun part was learning to read Hebrew from the *Torah*. This was a herculean effort for me. I was assigned to *Haftarah Tazria*, the *Haftarah* portion from 2 Kings 4:42–44; 5:1–19. *Haftarah*, translated from the Hebrew, means "conclusion."[4] *The Shengold Jewish Encyclopedia* provides a lucid definition of *Haftarah*, noting that it is the "section from the Prophets recited at the conclusion of the reading from the **Torah**, or Five Books of Moses, on the **Sabbath**, holidays, and during afternoon services on fast days."[5] My brother too had a *bar mitzvah* in the Reform synagogue, and his portion, *Haftarah Kedoshim*, was taken from Ezekiel 22:1–19. The prophet spoke about the sins of the people and the judgment from the son of man. My brother's *Haftarah* portion was a lesson that I would remember for a lifetime.

I am wearing the traditional *kippah* and *tallit* (Heb., head covering and prayer shawl) that I wore for my *bar mitzvah*. The photograph was taken at my mother's apartment in the spring of 1977.

4. See Schreiber et al., eds., *Shengold Jewish Encyclopedia*, 99.
5. Schreiber et al., eds., *Shengold Jewish Encyclopedia*, 99.

HOLOCAUST MEMORIES

My Jewish education began at the age of five in the Reform synagogue, and although my parent's divorced when I was nine years old,
my mother desired that her two sons continue to receive a Jewish
education, enforcing mandatory attendance at Sunday school every
week at the synagogue. Moreover, I learned about the atrocities
committed towards the Jewish people. Being exposed to graphic
pictures from the concentration camps, coupled with a deeply profound experience from the Sunday school teacher's morning class,
enabled me to synthesize the genocidal atrocities that were committed towards the Jewish people. For example, during a morning class,
this synagogue teacher read excerpts from the late Elie Wiesel's book
Night.[6] This teacher from the synagogue inspired me to purchase
and read this book in young adulthood. Every time that I reread
this book, tears of sorrow leap from my eyes. This memoir fosters
overwhelming grief and sadness within my soul. For Wiesel brought
me closer to the Holocaust than ever before as a young man.

While growing up in Queens, New York, I recall a Jewish man
and always noticed the green tattoo on his arm, which identified
Jews in the concentration camps, for the latter were indeed painful
remnants from the Holocaust. I had the wonderful opportunity to
know an older Jewish woman, a Holocaust survivor. She was kind
and personified a matriarchal figure while growing up as a Reform
Jew.

ADVENTUROUS UNDERTAKINGS

Growing up in a divorced home involved my mother waking up
at 4:30 a.m. to clean the house. She always had a good meal for
my brother and me after a long day on her feet working full-time
in the retail clothing industry. My mother had incredible strength
and stamina to raise two boys as a single parent. Growing up loving
sports, especially football, I spent time with friends and played in a
football league on the weekends. I remember my two-wheel Raleigh

6. See Wiesel, *Night*.

bicycle and loved riding around the Queens neighborhood. As an adventurous young kid, I remember setting up a ramp by my house to jump with this bicycle and enjoyed watching the motorcycle daredevil Evil Knievel on television. He inspired me to partake in daring stunts with this bicycle. Moreover, I loved to play on the vast green lawns outside my apartment building. My fun was spoiled when I saw a man in a green uniform yelling with his fist in the air, "Get off the lawn!" I always kept all the shifts of the doormen busy. I kept playing on the lawn, and again and again a different doorman would chase me off. If I couldn't play outside, my foot would kick a ball in the long, narrow hallway of the apartment floor. Warnings of my activity came in the form of an apartment door bursting open. After I saw a head peek out of the apartment door, I would exercise my right as a young kid and calmly state with brazen confidence, "I am sorry."

I was a young boy who loved to laugh and have fun, and soon found that ringing the doorbells in the apartment building and running down the steps was an experience of adventure. One day, I took off down the steps after ringing the doorbells. Furthermore, I ran down the stairs like the building was on fire, and took a turn in the stairwell, which was a lesson for my foul play. As I grabbed the wooden rail it was split in half, and as a result I tumbled forward and was propelled down the stairs, landing on my head on the stairwell floor. My mother rushed home immediately from work and took me to the emergency room, where I was diagnosed with a concussion. I learned my lesson that day in the stairwell. This injury was another lesson that I would remember for a lifetime.

TRAINING FOR ADVERSITY

I began lifting weights after I was inspired by a camp counselor during summer camp. I began pumping iron four to five days per week and found the muscle and fitness magazines to be inspirational. As a natural athlete, I found bodybuilding to be a challenging hobby. Being an active adolescent, it turned out to be more expensive to feed me than to put clothes on my back. Bodybuilders like Dave

Draper and Mike Katz fueled my being with determination to lift and be strong. These were some of my bodybuilding heroes from the 1970s and I greatly admired their commitment and dedication to build their physiques. The rigors of full-time school and training at the gym in the evenings taught me about diet, nutrition, and self-discipline. Another important muscle which I had to deal with was my mind and emotions, for I was about to embark upon an experience that would inspire and transform my life for years to come. Experiencing emotional discomfort from my parent's divorce, I was having trouble getting along with them and recall working with a counselor. He was a kind older man who represented a father figure to me. After arriving home from World War II, my counselor returned to school because he desired an education. This kind older man taught me about the gift of education. This was another lesson that I would remember for a lifetime.

My brother, Todd, worked at my father's printing brokerage firm in New York City. He got married in 1982 and seemed to be able to make a life for himself. My parent's divorce significantly affected my grades at school. Even though I had a lot of friends, it was difficult to concentrate and perform in my academic studies. As an athlete, I found great joy playing dodgeball during physical education class. I was always picked first by my fellow classmates for the dodgeball team because I threw the ball with accuracy and strength on the court. When I wasn't hitting home runs over the school fence during physical education class, my time after school was spent practicing with the high school students on the varsity soccer team. As a young man who excelled at sports, I would acquire deeper sense of meaning to this Jewish rite of passage of a *bar mitzvah*, and later on in young adulthood this would redefine that childhood yearning to know who and what God is when I inquisitively looked out that window in search of deity.

A family portrait taken of me, my mother, and brother Todd in our apartment.

Todd and me at his wedding in New York City, spring 1982.

LESSON IN ACTION

When we wonder about the presence of the almighty God, he begins to move in our lives below the threshold of awareness (see Phil

1:6). Remember that God is near and more in control than we can ever think or imagine. Jeremiah 23:23–24 states:

> "*Am* I a God near at hand," says the LORD,
> "And not a God afar off?
> Can anyone hide himself in secret places,
> So I shall not see him?" says the LORD;
> "Do I not fill heaven and earth?" says the LORD.

2

Chronicles of Self-Reliance

Blessed *is* the nation whose God *is* the Lord,
The people He has chosen as His own inheritance.

—Ps 33:12

HOLY LAND EXCURSION

My parents were hard-working people who tried their very best to provide for their children. My father was a wealthy printing executive who generously showered me with the material prizes of the time. For instance, I had expensive name-brand clothes, jewelry, automobiles, and audio equipment. Although my father was affluent and provided well for me, I experienced emptiness in the core of my being. Therefore the toys, gifts, money, and material possessions did not fill this void in my heart. One of the biggest accomplishments while growing up was earning enough money to purchase a plane ticket to Israel. My counselor recommended that I pursue a summer program on a kibbutz, a "communal settlement in **Israel.**[1] He wanted me to learn self-reliance in a foreign country and thought this would be a positive experience for my emotional and spiritual growth. The international flight departed from John F. Kennedy International Airport, bound for Ben Gurion InternationalAirport in Israel. My counselor and his wife saw me depart at the airport. His final parting words to me as I prepared to board the plane were, "Gregg, you are on your own." My former counselor's words personified that inevitable moment in life, namely, a time to learn and experience the inalienable right of self-reliance. This was a lesson that has lasted for a lifetime.

This Jewish college student from Queens, New York, was on his own, inside a steel machine bound for Israel. Upon arriving at Ben Gurion International Airport, an Israeli man from the kibbutz summer program was sent to the airport to meet us, and I was greeted by several volunteers who would be living and working with me on the kibbutz. We were shuttled away in the early morning hours and stopped at a restaurant on the way to the kibbutz. I made another journal entry which documented my arrival to Israel:

> There are twelve of us in the group. Our group leader appears to have a pleasant sense of humor and is very patient with our questions. We arrived at the kibbutz on Tuesday morning at 5:00 a.m. We were awakened at 9:45 a.m. My roommates and I cleaned up the room and tossed around a football. We had the day off. I took a twenty-minute walk around the kibbutz, saw livestock, and got fitted for my work clothes.

CHICKEN AEROBICS

My living quarters on the kibbutz were cramped as there were three single beds in the room. My roommate was a college student from a university on the East Coast, while the other roommate lived and worked in Manhattan. The window had a wood shutter equipped with a long pole that was used to keep the sun out of the room. There wasn't central air conditioning and my body sweated profusely as

---

1. See Schreiber et al., eds., *Shengold Jewish Encyclopedia*, 156.

I learned to live in this small room far away from home. Life on this rural, agrarian settlement would require a type of work that was indeed different than pumping iron or playing sports. We were quickly assigned work duties on the kibbutz, while my roommate and I received our first work orders; namely, we were assigned to assist with caging the chickens. Upon entering the large building after midnight, I observed hundreds of chickens running aimlessly in a frenzied state. The temperature was hot and the stench of the chickens invaded my nostrils at a ferocious speed. My journal documented this late-night industrious experience:

> As I write this, I have to get ready to wake my two room-
> mates so we could be at work by 12:45 a.m. at the chicken
> house. Our job was to cage many, many chickens. The
> next night we had the shift from 2:30 a.m. to 4:45 a.m.
> After we finished, my roommate and I went for coffee,
> and then back to the room where we collapsed into our
> beds at around 6:30 a.m. He has been a great roommate.
> We made it our point to stick together. He has really
> helped me through some tough moments.

The kibbutz workers instructed us to grab hold of the chickens and place several of them in a metal structure which had numerous cages. We worked most of the night caging chickens, while the sweat flew off my body like water from the majestic Niagara Falls. From this late-night industrious kibbutz experience, I coined the whole experience "chicken aerobics." We left the warehouse smelling like chickens and walked back to our living quarters. I remember being physically exhausted after this experience, for the lack of sleep caused me to laugh like a drunken man who had just come off the battlefield.

KIBBUTZNIK TO TOURIST

The rest of my stay at the kibbutz included working in the kitchen and the dining room, and picking apples from the trees. After a long, hard day's work, I enjoyed swimming in the pool, while other days were spent visiting the serene Banias Waterfall. I worked hard during my stay on this kibbutz, and as a temporary kibbutz worker I worked every day except Saturday. The state of Israel suspended all work on Saturday, for this day was the Jewish Sabbath. With that said, I and my fellow American college students, who had traveled halfway around the world to see the state of Israel, felt dismayed because our schedule prevented us from doing so. I recall talking to my father on the telephone about wanting to see the rest of this country and the historic sites of antiquity. As a gift, my father gave me a two-week tour of Israel for completing almost two years of college.

I remember leaving the kibbutz and boarding a bus for Jerusalem. The bus ride proved to be an interesting experience. First, there wasn't air conditioning on this trip to Jerusalem. Second, the bus abruptly came to a halt while Israeli army medics rushed through the corridor of the bus and provided medical attention for a woman. The air was stale and it seemed like the sultry humidity may have been to blame for this woman's health issues. Upon arriving in Jerusalem, my father's instructions were to walk to a specific hotel because I had a reservation for a room. Feeling like a stranger in a strange land, my appearance mirrored a refugee who had just fled his home with numerous belongings. Holding multiple suitcases and bags, I did the one thing my father told me to do, for he said, "God gave you a mouth; use it!" I asked an Israeli man if he could help me locate my hotel. With broken English, he provided directions and escorted me through a tunnel that led to the other side of the street. At this moment, I felt like that boy who gazed out the window looking for a supreme being. From this experience, I learned that God was visible to me and reached out to me through the kindness of a stranger. This too was another lesson that I would remember for a lifetime.

LESSON IN ACTION

When we are looking for God, we need to look at the people we interact with in our day-to-day lives, for it is here where Scripture reminds, "Do not forget to entertain strangers, for by so *doing* some have unwittingly entertained angels" (Heb 13:2). Can you think about people or events in your life that transcend human reason, while bordering the divine? Take a moment to reflect on this statement. And remember, God places people in our lives to guide, challenge, and encourage us on this wonderful journey called life.

3

Failing, but Persevering

The hand of the diligent will rule,
But the lazy *man* will be put to forced labor.
—PROV 12:24

QUEST FOR JEWISH IDENTITY

I felt like I was living in civilization again; air-conditioned rooms, great food, and swimming at the hotel. After my short stay at this hotel, I rendezvoused with the tour group. The tour guide was a middle-aged Jewish man and we traveled around with him on the tour bus visiting many historic sites throughout Israel. I appreciated the opportunity to see many of these historic sites. However, I wasn't excited that my only option to use the bathroom was an outhouse which was located near the main road. Eventually, the driver stopped the tour bus and pointed with his finger to where I needed to go. There was not a bathroom in sight! The gates of Joshua were about to open, the Israeli man pointed, and I ran. "Wait a minute," I thought to myself. I saw two wooden makeshift stalls grouped together and sprinted inside of one of them with urgency, saying to myself, "Where's the porcelain throne?" I looked down and saw makeshift toilets in the dirt, which were molded together to resemble a toilet seat. Looking down this hole produced flaring nostrils, while my emotional composure erupted like Mount St. Helens, thus overwhelming my brain with intense fear. My inner self-talk erupted, "I am not doing this!" And I sprinted back to the safety of the tour bus, while the rush of the adrenalin enabled me to wait to use the lavatory upon my return to the hotel. Overall, the tour of Israel helped me to understand my Jewish roots, for I saw historic sites that were considered landmarks. For instance, across the street from the *Knesset* (Israel's parliament building) was a menorah, a symbol of the Jewish holiday Hanukkah. The *Shengold Jewish Encyclopedia* defines this Jewish holiday as

> The Feast of Dedication and Lights, which falls on the 25th of **Kislev** and lasts for eight days. It marks the re-dedication of the **Temple** by Judah **Maccabee** in 165 B.C.E. after his victory over the Syrians who had defiled the sanctuary.[1]

I am swinging from a tree at the Banias Waterfall. The tour of Israel visited the place where I enjoyed discretionary time off from my work duties on the kibbutz.

---

1. Schreiber et al., eds., *Shengold Jewish Encyclopedia*, 103.

The tour of Israel visited Caesarea, which is located on the Mediterranean coast. I am standing by the vestige of a structure.

After the tour of Israel concluded, I stayed in Tel Aviv for a few days and departed back to New York City with a sense of accomplishment. I had learned about self-reliance in a foreign country, my knowledge of Judaism was strengthened, and I acquired personal growth from the experience.

TIME OF TRANSITION

I arrived home to my apartment in Fort Lee, New Jersey, the first city which separated Manhattan and New Jersey by the George Washington Bridge. It is worth repeating, five weeks of self-reliance in Israel was an invigorating experience, for I had learned about my Jewish faith, lived and worked on a kibbutz for several weeks, and experienced the historic Jewish sites of antiquity. After completing two years of college, I had a few more semesters remaining in order to complete my Associate of Arts degree. The last two semesters before I left for Israel, as well as my arrival home after this trip, were quite difficult. For instance, I found myself involved in the world of partying. Late-night parties filled the void in my heart and school-work didn't seem important. Wanting to "party" and do my own thing in life, I neglected my schoolwork and as a result received failing grades. My lifestyle of debauchery and neglecting to study caused me to fail out of school.

Upon returning home from Israel, I decided to take some time off from college and worked as a messenger for my father's printing brokerage firm in midtown Manhattan. The job responsibilities entailed delivering packages around Manhattan to the printing clients. I remember numerous subway and bus rides around Manhattan. These tasks were monotonous for me, while the highlight of the job was buying and eating hot dogs from the street vendors.

One day, while walking in Manhattan, I looked across the street and recognized a heavyweight boxing champion strolling down Fifth Avenue with shopping bags. The gift of education which the counselor had planted within my soul was much like a heavyweight shot at the boxing title, for I was about to embark upon a deeply meaningful quest which redefined my life for decades.

EDUCATIONAL YEARNING

My father told me that he would help me return to school in order to complete my Associate of Arts degree. At this time, I relocated from New Jersey to central Vermont and worked for an organization. My job duties consisted of performing light administrative duties around their office. There was a private university about two miles from my house and I inquired about taking courses towards my associate's degree. The most affordable option for me was to take courses at a reduced rate in their Adult Degree Program. I needed some classes to complete the associate's degree and recall taking classes at this university. I developed an aptitude for the social sciences, receiving several As for courses in psychology. The other course that I needed for the associate's degree was college algebra, and although I spent many hours on the math assignments, I received only a C for the course.

I remember opening up a large brown package addressed to me in Vermont. Inside the package was the degree from the two-year college. I did it! Now I could enroll in full-time studies at the university, for the main campus was a military college. Although my plans were not to enlist in the military, I learned that the main campus, Norwich University, allowed the civilian students to integrate with the cadets in the educational milieu. Resonating throughout my soul was the uncertain question, "What do I study in school?"

I successfully demonstrated to myself that I earned a degree, faithfully studied, read, and took the tests in the courses. Little did I know that the biggest test ahead in life was not listed in the university curriculum.

LESSON IN ACTION

Is there uncertainty about the direction you are headed in your life? Are you anaesthetizing your emotions with work, food, smoking, or alcohol? Consider nourishing your soul with the Word of God. Are you at an impasse in life? The psalmist reveals the solution for navigating through the ambiguous valleys in life, and instructs God's people to remember:

> Your word *is* a lamp to my feet
> And a light to my path.
> I have sworn and confirmed
> That I will keep Your righteous judgments. (Ps 119:105–6)

4

The Sun Still Shines

A Call to God

Let my cry come before You, O Lord;
Give me understanding according to Your word.
Let my supplication come before You;
Deliver me according to Your word.

—Ps 119:169–70

UNEXPECTED NEWS

I recall the phone call one evening around the mid part of November 1988. Upon returning home from working out at the gym across the street from my apartment, I had several messages on the answering machine regarding news from my family. I began wondering if something had happened to my elderly grandmother in Brooklyn. I never would have suspected to hear the forthcoming yet tragic news which radiated waves of fear. I learned that my twenty-eight-year-old brother, Todd, had been in a serious automobile accident. Learning this moved me to emphatically cry aloud, "He has a sixteen-month-old baby!" My father was vacationing on the other side of the globe when he called me from the airport. He spoke with me by telephone about this accident and remarked, "Let's hope Brother makes it." My friends arranged for my airline ticket home the following morning. Feeling shaken by the news, I stayed at my friend's home that evening. I vividly recall the airplane flight home from Vermont to LaGuardia Airport in New York City. My flight departed around 6:50 in the morning and I had a lot of sadness during the plane ride home to New York. I had my university notebook with me on the airplane and opened up that notebook, pouring out my soul to God. I didn't know who God was or even how to pray. With a pen in my left hand and my heart open to God, I began to write from the depths of my being. As I wrote in this notebook, I recall seeing the sun rising from outside the airplane window, for the warmth of the sun comforted my soul as I continued writing in the journal:

A Cry to God; 7 a.m., November 19, 1988

I feel like I want to cry. I am still in shock over the accident. I know that Todd knows how much I love him and need him. Last night, I prayed to everyone, Jesus, God and to any supreme being who was over me. Todd is taking his own path right now. I must respect his path, but I am in constant prayer, much like a track coach who keeps running alongside his runner, offering nourishment, love, and support. Everyone is praying for him and I am sending as much spiritual energy to him so he can get well. He is too young to die. God and Jesus know that Todd's faith is in his and the Lord's hands. The sun is coming up from behind me. Again, I request that all the warmth from the sun be beamed into Todd giving him warmth and love. I brought something for him; a statue of Moses, my *Chai*, and a *Magen David* [Heb., Life and Star of David]. *Chai* means life, and I want Todd to have it. He deserves it, loves it, and needs it. He's too good to let go to the heavens right now. If there are any of my relatives there or with Todd right now, I say to them, Papa Harry, Uncle Murray, and Nana Ceal, please behold him, my brother. Tell him how much everyone loves him. Please don't let him die. He's all I got. I need him. His wife and baby need him, and most of all, society needs him because he has a lot to give. It's not his time yet to fly to heaven. Leave him on earth. Pray for him, and please keep him alive. Todd, if you can hear me right now, I want to tell you to keep breathing and fighting. With life there is hope. My heart is with your soul and your soul is in my heart. We are connected and I want to pass you my love, strength, and life energies. Everyone is rooting for you. Hold tight and keep the hope alive. We all have to be strong to get through this. You need to be strong to fight and come out of your coma. We have been through some rough times together. And we fought a lot. All in all, I love you Todd more than anyone in the world. You are my only brother. We grew up together. We have seen each other's ups and downs. Please don't die. I respect your path that you are on. I want you to take my strength. It's full of love, nurturance, and hope. I got you a surprise which I want to give you. I brought a statue of Moses with me who will be by your side. I figured if he could part the Red Sea and free his people from bond-age, I think he can use his prophet wisdom to heal. One commandment sticks out Todd and this is to honor thy brother. I honor you, respect you, and love you. We are all connected. I am hoping that our prayers are answered by the Lord almighty God. He is almighty. But you know something, so is the human spirit, and will. It is just as strong because it can perform remarkable feats of incom-prehensible miracles. Till I see you, Todd. Please hold tight and know that I am here for you.

Dear God and Jesus Christ. Please watch over Todd until I get to the hospital. Sending him my prayers and praying for the swelling on his head to go down.

PRAISE REPORT: 10 P.M., NOVEMBER 19, 1988

I am still praying, thank you God and Jesus Christ. You are watching over him. And I take another moment to pray again: Dear God, almighty Lord, king of the uni-verse, and Jesus Christ. Please continue to watch over my brother. I love him so much God and Jesus. I ask you to give me strength and hope, for I am only human God and not immune of enduring pain. I see things differently now, God and Jesus. I have a responsibility to myself, my family, and friends to be strong. I want to place a statue of Moses with my brother at his bedside. I figured if Moses led his people out of oppression and received his instructions from You, then I know Moses will be praying to God, too. Please, may you watch and give Todd, me, and my family strength and hope. *Shema Yisrael, Adonai Eloheinu, Adonai Echad.* "Hear, O Israel: The LORD our God, the LORD *is* one!" [Heb. transliteration, Deut 6:4]. Amen.

CRITICAL, BUT ALIVE

We arrived at the hospital in Westchester, New York, the following day. Todd was in critical condition in the intensive care unit. His head was swollen like a bowling ball as he lay in the hospital bed hooked up to wires. With a fractured skull, his brain was deprived of oxygen and Todd sustained a severe head injury resulting in brain stem damage. Moreover, he sustained a crushed sternum and was heavily sedated to keep the swelling on his brain reduced. His body temperature at one point soared past 104 degrees in the hospital. This was due to damage to the area of the brain that controls bodily temperature. Todd's condition in the intensive care unit improved enough for him to be transported to a head injury rehabilitation facility. As his condition slowly improved, my family and I noticed small blessings with each passing day. For instance, immobilized in a wheelchair, Todd raised his hand and acknowledged his family. At one point, he was able to take a pen and write his name on the pad of paper. Although the penmanship was illegible, this represented hope that Todd was on the road to recovery.

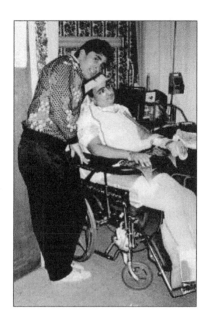

Following a lengthy hospital stay, Todd was transferred to a head injury rehabilitation facility. This photograph was taken not too long after his arrival at the facility.

At the head injury rehabilitation facility, Todd relearned how to write his name on a pad of paper.

HUMANITARIAN DEED

According to my father and mother, a doctor and a nurse were traveling together and stopped at the accident scene to provide medical help for my brother. This was reflected in the news article, "Roadside surgery may have saved life."[1] The physician and the nurse were indeed Good Samaritans and could have continued driving, but were moved with compassion to offer medical aid. In Luke 10, Jesus describes a man who was wounded from being beaten and robbed by thieves. This man, like Todd, sustained injuries from an unfortunate event. Jesus describes a Samaritan as having great compassion for this injured man. Before the Samaritan arrived on the scene, a Levite and a priest had passed by and ignored the injured man (see Luke 10:30–34). I began to see and experience God working through people; the Israeli man helping me to locate the hotel, my former counselor, and finally the medical doctor and the nurse all represented God's way of reaching out to me and my brother in times of distress. After arriving home in central Vermont, I returned to a normal life routine, hoping that there would be better days ahead after Todd's automobile accident and severe traumatic brain injury.

LESSON IN ACTION

Life can throw unexpected circumstances or tragedies into our lives. We never know if today will be our last minute or hour alive. It may be the last time that we see our loved ones. Please consider making peace with them, while considering the essence of time. James writes:

> Come now, you who say, "Today or tomorrow we will go to such and such a city, spend a year there, buy and sell, and make a profit"; whereas you do not know what *will happen* tomorrow. For what is your life? It is even a vapor that appears for a little time and then vanishes away. (Jas 4:13–14)

1 Golding, "Roadside Surgery May Have Saved Life," A3.

It is wise to call your loved ones and tell them that you love them. Make it a daily habit to perform kind deeds for people in need. Acts 20:35 teaches, "I have shown you in every way, by laboring like this, that you must support the weak. And remember the words of the Lord Jesus, that He said, 'It is more blessed to give than to receive.'"

5

Tragedy to Triumph

The end of a thing *is* better than its beginning;
The patient in spirit *is* better than the proud in spirit.
—ECCL 7:8

FAITHFUL SERVICE

I returned home to Vermont facing the next challenge; what major do I declare at the university? As a full-time student, I was entitled to one free counseling session per week, and eventually pursued counseling with my psychology professor from summer school. When I contacted him about pursuing counseling, he told me that he was sorry to hear about my brother's accident and said that if he counseled me I wouldn't be able to take courses with him at the university. Bound by a professional ethic and duty, I agreed to work with him. This counselor at the university was a kind older man, much like the counselor who worked with me after the divorce of my parents. As we worked together, he assisted me with declaring a major. He learned that my father was in the printing business and thumbed through the Norwich University catalogue with special attention given to the communications curriculum. This university psychologist helped me understand myself and assisted me with processing my brother's tragic automobile accident. I poured out my soul to this man and, thankfully, God found a wise man to counsel, direct, and comfort me, for this tender soul was a fine example of how God works through others' hearts on this journey called life. The aforementioned encounter with the psychologist reminds us to seek counsel from the Lord. Proverbs 19:20–21 states:

> Listen to counsel and receive instruction,
> That you may be wise in your latter days.
>
> There are many plans in a man's heart,
> Nevertheless the LORD's counsel—that will stand.

Although I wasn't a Christian during this time, God was planting the seeds and preparing me to receive his son, Jesus Christ. God used both counselors in my life to provide safety and well-being, therefore I learned to appreciate the proverb, "Where *there is* no counsel, the people fall; But in the multitude of counselors *there is* safety" (Prov 11:14). I pursued my coursework at Norwich University with an intense zeal to succeed, and the counselor helped me to grow emotionally, while integrating the academic coursework into my psychological well-being. As the semester progressed, I earned academic accolades for the Dean's List. Soon thereafter came writing accolades for my academic work in the journalism classes. My journalism professor awarded me for the Best Off-Campus New Story for the year, 1989–1990, and I earned the Second Miler Award for the academic school year. This was awarded to the student who goes the extra distance in his or her schoolwork. Moreover, the journalism professor offered me an Off-Campus Editor position with *The Guidon* campus newspaper. I was responsible for covering the off-campus news stories in the surrounding communities of central Vermont.

An international event that was held at the campus was, indeed, the pinnacle of my journalism studies in the undergraduate program of communications. The university that I attended participated in the Partners of the Americas organization and the Honduran president,

Rafael Leonardo Callejas, attended the twenty-fifth anniversary commemoration at Norwich University.[1] The front-page news story for the *Guidon* stated, "In greeting President Rafael Leonardo Callejas, Norwich President W. Russell Todd said that it was a privilege to celebrate the 25th anniversary at Vermont College, which hosts participants who travel to Montpelier regularly to study business development and agriculture."[2] Todd announced, "Mr. President someday may your successor be a Norwich graduate."[3]

I wrote the *Guidon* news story for this historic commemorative event, while security was strictly enforced on the campus. For example, in addition to the Honduran president visiting the university, we had the Vermont governor, Madeleine Kunin, in attendance, and I was required to undergo a security clearance in order to enter the building. As the staff photographer accompanied me towards the Vermont College building, he received a telephone call that his National Guard unit was activated and without hesitation placed a thirty-five-millimeter camera in my hand, instructing me to take pictures of the event. I wrote the story for the campus newspaper and took pictures of Honduran President Rafael Leonardo Callejas's visit to Norwich University. It was, indeed, a unique honor to be a part of this unprecedented event at Norwich University.

FRUITS OF LABOR

I continued to excel in my courses at the university, while many late nights were spent reading, studying, and writing papers and news stories. I worked with fervor, striving to be the person God intended me to be in life. One morning, I noticed a piece of paper in the student mailbox. This was an invitation informing me that I would be awarded academic accolades at the fall convocation. I had served faithfully and learned alongside the cadets in the classes at the university. Nonetheless, I wasn't a cadet in training for the Army, Air Force, Marines, Navy, or the Coast Guard. I was a Jew from Queens,

1. Grossman, "Honduran President Visits Campus," front page.
2. Grossman, "Honduran President Visits Campus," front page.
3. Grossman, "Honduran President Visits Campus," front page.

New York, who had just endured the biggest battle of my life. As I endured and survived the deep pain of Todd's accident, I was impressed by God to return back to school because this was the desire of my heart before this family tragedy. Hence the psalmist's words:

Delight yourself also in the LORD,
And he shall give you the desires of your heart. (Ps 37:4)

I began to see the desires of my heart fulfilled at convocation an event that honored the cadets for their military and meritorious deeds of academic excellence. Although a civilian student, I participated in the event and would be receiving coveted academic awards at this ceremony. The convocation program described the two awards that I received at this event. For example, the Wagner Prize in Communications is presented "annually to the communications majors with the highest quality-point averages in their first six semesters of full-time study and whose writing, speaking, and dealing with language are outstanding."[4] I received first prize for this award and was presented with a certificate and check for my academic endeavors. Moreover, I earned the Presidential Fellowship for the Humanities Division. The convocation program states,

Seven seniors selected on evidence of exceptional scholastic ability and academic performance. The Presidential Fellows constitute an academic advisory committee to the President and the Dean, and meet periodically with them and with the Academic Affairs Committee of the Trustees to discuss matters of common concern in the academic program of the University.[5]

Along with the Presidential Fellowship award winners, I was selected to represent the university at a dinner with representatives from the New England Association of Secondary Colleges (NEASC). This event was another unique honor for me during my undergraduate studies.

During the last semester of study, there was uncertainty about the kind of work that I would perform after graduation. Was I to

4. Norwich University, *Convocation Program,* 4.
5. Norwich University, *Convocation Program,* 4.

enter my father's business and earn a lot of money? Or should I pursue graduate work in my passion, psychology and counseling? Christ clearly spoke through the lips of my counselor one day in the counseling session. This counselor asked, "For what profit is it to a man if he gains the whole world, and loses his own soul?" (Matt 16:26a). Those words resonated through my soul and became pivotal seeds for me, spiritually; namely, they were profound words that I would remember for a lifetime.

THE FINISH LINE

I graduated summa cum laude on May 18, 1991 from Norwich University. As a civilian student attending a military college, I learned about self-discipline and service to the community. God had taken a broken-hearted Jewish man, healed his mind from family tragedy, and restored him for service. I developed a wonderful working relationship with my professors from the university and was blessed to know another kind older man who was my neighbor in Vermont. I went grocery shopping for him at the store and learned to serve God by serving my neighbor. The *Torah* captures the heartbeat of the interpersonal enterprise, stating, "You shall not take vengeance, nor bear any grudge against the children of your people, but you shall love your neighbor as yourself: I *am* the LORD" (Lev 19:18). Finally, I made frequent trips to visit my brother at the head injury rehabilitation facility and with each trip I noticed small improvements. It is worth repeating, Todd was able to write his name, and I learned to look for the good in these situations. Moreover, he retained a sense of humor and long-term memory, and when I asked him to recite our father's office telephone number, Todd whispered the number with soft, unintelligible speech. He remembered people's names from growing up. However, if I asked Todd about an event from ten minutes ago, he wouldn't be able to remember, for his short-term memory damage was due to the severe traumatic brain injury, a repercussion that I would relate to in the unforeseeable future.

I am wearing my cap and gown at Norwich University's commencement
ceremony, which was held on May 18, 1991 in Northfield, Vermont.

THE JOURNEY TO GOD

After graduating from Norwich University, I decided to relocate
to South Florida to be with my father. I had received my entrance
letter into the Master of Science program at Nova Southeastern
University (formerly Nova University) and was scheduled to begin
graduate studies in mental health counseling. My former counselor
from the university taught me a lifelong lesson: "Be true to yourself
and good things will happen." After seeing Todd at the head injury
rehabilitation facility, I embarked upon the next leg of the journey.
With the exception of my father and his wife, I didn't know anyone
in South Florida, and recall praying to God for direction with this
next step in life. I stayed with my father and his wife at their home
in South Florida.

At the time, I experienced God speaking to me through the
Bible on the radio. For example, I heard an evangelist on the radio
while driving my car around the neighborhood, and he preached the
Word of God with conviction. I recall hearing a wonderful sermon
by the late Dr. Adrian Rogers which was broadcasted on Trinity
Broadcasting Network. He described the Spirit-filled life and stated,

"Glory outweighs trouble when you believe in the inward and the invisible. When we persevere over pressure and triumph over trial, we live. Invisible sources require our best demand."[6] I learned from this minister that I had persevered from a trial in life, namely, the tragic car accident of my older sibling. Below the threshold of conscious awareness lay the grace of God, for this enabled me to rise above the embarrassment of failing out of college, while instilling inner comfort from the devastating pain from my brother's severe traumatic brain injury. Furthermore, this inner strength and leading of the Lord represented an unconscious leading by his Spirit. My journal entry in South Florida demonstrated that God was leading me to his son, Jesus Christ. On July 14, 1991, I wrote:

> The inward and the invisible I sense, reflects at least in my mind, a higher being graced by the Lord Jesus Christ. While growing up, especially at home and at the synagogue, I was never exposed to the teachings of Jesus and his disciples. The greatest insights in life are sometimes crystalized and synthesized best through reflection. As a student at the university, I was moved by an indefatigable, spiritual force. It wasn't the body that moved me, but the spirit.

THE EMPTY VOID

I had embraced secular humanism and became a well-read, informed citizen in the world. Although bright, intelligent, and skilled with writing and expressing the English language, I still felt a lingering void in my heart, for there was a sincere hunger and thirst for something from God. My plans were to earn a Master of Science degree in mental health counseling and return to school for doctoral work. A notable aspiration; however, God had other plans for me in South Florida. I had worked full-time, earning two Bs in graduate school, and when I wrote my former counselor and professor from the university about these grades, his letter praised my

6. Date and title of sermon unknown. Many of Dr. Rogers' messages are found at Love Worth Finding Ministries, lwf.org. Used by Permission.

ability to work full-time and complete graduate work in the mental health counseling program. I was working full-time at a business to support myself while studying for the master's degree, and remember studying for an exam in the Introduction to Counseling class. I recall talking to a man at this business. When I told him about this forthcoming test, he lamented, "Brother, I am being tested every day." I soon learned that my biggest test was not with human ideas, thoughts, or theories. Rather, my biggest test would be my faith in God.

One afternoon in the summer before graduate classes started, I visited the university, walked around the campus, and stopped to ask a gentleman for help to locate the campus library. I told him about being a prospective graduate student and being new to the Fort Lauderdale community. I developed a rapport and a friendship with this graduate student. Moreover, he was a vital help to me during the adjustment of relocating to Florida. With that said, I made a connection with someone while adapting to this tropical environment. With the challenges that lay ahead, God foreknew that I was going to need a friend.

LESSON IN ACTION

Education and the acquisition of wisdom and material provision are indeed blessings! However, Solomon, the wisest man in the world, had wealth, power, prestige, and wisdom. Remember, although Solomon seemed to have it together, he became filled with cynicism later in life. Have you reached a point in your life where you think you "have it all" and believe that this still isn't enough? Take a lesson from Solomon, who became a rich man when he understood:

> The fear of the LORD *is* the beginning of knowledge,
> *But* fools despise wisdom and instruction. (Prov 1:7)

6

You Can Run, but You Can't Hide

He who dwells in the secret place of the Most High
Shall abide under the shadow of the Almighty.

—Ps 91:1

DEHYDRATED SOUL

It was a beautiful sunny day in South Florida and I recall relaxing at the condominium pool where I had rented a room from a graduate student. I had a small radio with me at the pool which sat on the brusque tile floor beside the chase lounge. The drive for learning psychology and philosophy were depleted at this point in life. Nevertheless, hearing a radio minister talk about faith was like pouring cold water into a dehydrated spirit. On that day, I learned that "faith *comes* by hearing, and hearing by the word of God" (Rom 10:17).[1] The empty void in my heart became filled with something that I had never heard nor experienced in life. I had a *bar mitzvah*, graduated with highest honors from the university, and was thoughtful of my

---

1. Kenneth E. Hagin, *Faith Seminar of the Air* (radio program), 1991.

neighbor. I learned that although God does appreciate good deeds and works in life, Scripture teaches, "For by grace you have been saved through faith, and that not of yourselves; *it is* the gift of God, not of works, lest anyone should boast" (Eph 2:8–9).

As I began to hear the Word of God, I felt comforted and enlightened throughout my whole being. Suffice to say this experience represented a powerful spiritual lesson from God, namely, that I am not only a mind and a physical body, but a spirit being. Years later, it was intriguing to reflect upon these journal entries, particularly after Todd's accident, for I was experiencing the leading of God. For example, the minister that I had heard on the radio at the condominium swimming pool cited Proverbs 20:27, "The spirit of a man *is* the lamp of the LORD, Searching all the inner depths of his heart."[2] At one point, I questioned my conviction and asked myself, "How can I be Jewish and believe in Jesus Christ?" Scripture comforted me about being Jewish and believing in the gospel. The apostle Paul writes, "For I am not ashamed of the gospel of Christ, for it is the power of God to salvation for everyone who believes, for the Jew first and also for the Greek" (Rom 1:16). I documented a journal entry that captured this deep yearning for Jesus Christ, while lying awake in bed:

> Lord Jesus, I pray you lay my soul to sleep. Please, my Savior, grant me entrance alongside your sheep. Have mercy on thine iniquities and transgressions of thine past. Please, Lord Jesus make peace within myself last. Must a man approach you with fear and a trembling face? Jesus Christ, O Lord, please grant me some grace. With every rolling tear and every tear in my heart, I sense if I accept you in my life, I can be born again, thus having a fresh start. You died for my sins in the Middle East. Man flogged you and treated you like a beast. I pray for your grace. I pray for the courage to accept you in my life.

2. Kenneth E. Hagin, *Faith Seminar of the Air* (radio program), 1991.

REBIRTH OF A WOUNDED JEW

I learned about the New Testament and developed a deep abiding faith and belief in Jesus Christ. When studying the Bible, particularly the New Testament, I began to understand who Jesus Christ was and why God sent him to the earth. Christ states:

> For God so loved the world that He gave His only begotten Son, that whoever believes in Him should not perish but have everlasting life. For God did not send His Son into the world to condemn the world, but that the world through Him might be saved. (John 3:16–17)

What I learned from the New Testament was never taught in the synagogue. I thought the *Torah*, also known as the Pentateuch, which includes the five books of Moses, was all I needed to know as a Jew. As my faith in God through his Son, Jesus Christ, grew, the Bible stated that I must be born again in order to enter heaven (see John 3:3). At this time, there wasn't anyone around that I could talk to about spiritual matters. In March 1992, eight months after hearing about faith and Jesus Christ, I approached God with the heart of a child, reciting the Sinner's Prayer to the Lord on my knees in the condominium bedroom. Jesus Christ said in his Word that he would take me in. "All that the Father gives Me will come to Me, and the one who comes to Me I will by no means cast out" (John 6:37). As I recited the Sinner's Prayer to the Lord, I confessed with my mouth the Lord Jesus, truly and sincerely believing in my heart that God raised him from the dead. The apostle Paul writes, "But what does it say? 'The word is near you, in your mouth and in your heart' (that is, the word of faith which we preach): that if you confess with your mouth the Lord Jesus and believe in your heart that God has raised Him from the dead, you will be saved" (Rom 10:8–9).[3] As a Jewish believer in Christ, I know that Scripture emphasizes that God doesn't show partiality (Acts 10:34–35), especially "between Jewish and Gentile Christians." The Old and the New Testament

---

3. This is from my memory of the Sinner's Prayer which I prayed to receive the Lord, as found in a 1992 issue of *The Word of Faith* monthly magazine.

accentuate that salvation is available to all who will believe.[4] I truly believed in my heart that Jesus Christ is the Son of God and recognized that I needed Jesus Christ as Savior to mediate my case to God. Paul writes:

> For *there is* one God and one Mediator between God and men, *the* Man Christ Jesus, who gave Himself a ransom for all, to be testified in due time, for which I was appointed a preacher and an apostle—I am speaking the truth in Christ *and* not lying—a teacher of the Gentiles in faith and truth. (1 Tim 2:5–7)

RUNNING TOWARD GOD

On the morning of June 9, 1992, while jogging in the condominium complex, I was hit by a car, and learned later that I had made the mistake of not jogging against traffic in order for the cars to see me. The automobile hit me from behind while going close to forty miles per hour. I lost four pints of blood, sustained a severe concussion, resulting in sixteen stitches to my head, and shattered my left tibia and fibula, requiring emergency surgery to set the bones with hardware. I learned later that the man who had hit me was a new Christian, had a cellular phone in his car, and called the Florida Highway Patrol. They contacted an emergency medical helicopter, the Trauma Hawk, which airlifted me to a hospital in Broward County. I should have bled to death on that road. However, I fed my spirit with God's Word, received Jesus Christ as Lord, and therefore survived the accident. The greater one lives on the inside of me. John writes, "You are of God, little children, and have overcome them, because He who is in you is greater than he who is in the world" (1 John 4:4).

Although my mind has blocked out most of the trauma, I have residual memories from the accident. For example, I recall seeing an American flag and learned later that this was from the

---

4. Letter from Kenneth Hagin Ministries to Gregg Grossman, January 20, 1992. This was an excerpt and summarization from a letter I had written with questions about being Jewish and believing in Jesus Christ.

shirt of the paramedic who arrived at the accident scene. Second, I remember my college ring being pulled off my finger. Inside the ring was engraved Gregg Layne Grossman. I learned later that the ring identified me because my father's name and address were on file in the property management office. Third, my father informed me that I was in so much pain that he could hear my screams down the hallway of the hospital. Fourth, I recall my father and his wife by my side as the gurney moved down the long corridor. I saw the clock on my left and learned later that it was after 6:30 a.m. when the hospital personnel rolled me into surgery. The doctors waited for my condition to stabilize before they operated on the broken leg. Finally, I awoke slowly in the hospital bed and remember being told what had happened to me.

While recovering, I learned that the gentleman that talked with me on campus at graduate school came to see me in the hospital. I awoke one evening to find a note attached to the chair. This note from my friend said that he had come to see me but had to leave because he needed to be at work early the following morning. The man who hit me with his automobile came to visit me in the hospital and I shared about being a new-born Christian. This fellow believer brought me a new Walkman and told me that he was a fairly new believer in Jesus Christ. I recall lying in bed one evening and hearing that a man lying in a hospital bed adjacent to me had visitors from the Catholic Church. I heard Catholic prayers for the man, and without hesitation I reached for my Walkman and listened to a cassette tape from a Christian ministry. Listening to the Word of God comforted my injured body and soul while convalescing in the hospital.

FIGHTING FOR RECOVERY

After my condition improved at the hospital, I was sent to a rehabilitation facility towards the end of June 1992. My father worked for a company and one of his clients whom I had met before the accident was a minister. This kind minister arranged for his church to pack up my apartment belongings, which were placed in a storage room. I remember when this minister visited me in the rehabilitation facility. He brought me the Living Bible and concluded his visit with prayer, stating afterwards, "Gregg, I expect to hear good things from you." The first several days at the rehabilitation facility were exceedingly difficult. The pain in my left ankle became intense during the middle of the night. The pain was greater than the desire to sleep. I pulled the cord by my bed and alerted the nurse's station. The nurse came to my aid, gave me extra-strength Tylenol, and I was only able to sleep two hours that evening. The pain continued the following evening as I tried to sleep. Once again I pulled the cord, saw a nurse rush towards my hospital bed, and was given two tablets of extra-strength Tylenol for the intense pain. The following evening, the pain continued and once again I pulled the cord for medical aid. This time, the nurse came in and said she would call the doctor. Shortly afterwards, the nurse entered the room with a hypodermic needle. I carefully turned over in the bed as the nurse administered a shot of Demerol. The nurse entered the room the following day and informed me that the staples in my left ankle were ready to be removed, explaining that this was the reason for the discomfort. The doctor soon entered the room with clippers in his hand and told me that he was going to remove the staples in my left leg. Praying in the name of Jesus, I grabbed the side of the bed and held my Bible as the doctor began to remove the staples. As the doctor worked his way down my left ankle, one by one I saw each staple detach from my injured leg and heard a noise in the corner of the room because the staples hit the radiator with a forceful sound.

YEARNINGS IN THE DISTANCE

The day was July 4, 1992, and I finally rested from two difficult nights. I recall sitting in a wheelchair outside at the rehabilitation facility. Still feeling mentally impaired from the severe concussion, I was drowsy from the shot of Demerol and confined in this wheelchair. I recall seeing traffic about one hundred yards from the facility, and I wanted to be driving and back to a normal life routine. I recall thinking about my counselor and professors at the university. There were positive memories of the university and my friends from the Green Mountain State. I was able to express my faith as a Christian and found comfort journaling while sitting in the wheelchair outside at the rehabilitation facility:

> Today is Saturday, July 4, 1992. I am sitting outside the rehab facility. I still sit in a wheelchair with my left foot propped up. Memories of people in my past are coming back. I feel tired. I have been here for a week. I tire easily and my legs feel bruised and semi-numb from not walking. I feel a sense of gratitude to God for saving my life. I received a second chance to live; to grow up as a born again Christian. I love the Bible and I aspire to grow tall with pride as a new born Christian. I am proud of my new belief system. I pray every day in the name of Jesus Christ. I pray to the Father, for he is in heaven and boldly watching his children. I love my God and Jesus Christ. I love them with all of my heart. Both are magnified in my life. The Lord has sent me here to rest and regroup. He gave me another chance because I am a child of God. Also, I feel that God wants me to "preach the gospel to every creature" (Mark 16:15).

I am convalescing outside at the rehabilitation facility, July 1992.

REFLECTIONS OF HOPE

As I lay recovering from a traumatic brain injury, unable to walk, the anointing of God inspired me to write, for these poems reflected deep communion with the Lord. I recall a time of deep emotional pain about this accident. My head was woozy from the severe concussion and I was weak and unable to walk. I recall lying in bed reading through the book of Job. With a pen in my left hand, I managed to write two journal entries in a contemplative state:

I'm Coming Back

My God, I am alive. I breathe and move. Praise the Lord. I will fly high like the Phoenix Bird,[5] over the other side where it can shine bright. Do you know why? I am a child of God and have been raised from an abyss. The power of God and Jesus Christ are raising me up. My father hasn't abandoned me. God and Jesus are together. Both are almighty, life giving forces. I love them both. God shines bright to his children. Oh, praise the Lord, for he is alive and well, abiding in my spirit. I love Jesus. He has prepared a place and he is watching over me.

Man Endureth

In life, man endureth the wrath of his iniquities. Behold, throughout all of the pain, he is new creation in Christ (2 Cor 5:17). The shepherd searcheth the spirit of all believers. To live is to endure, however, to endure is to know that the Lord heareth my cry. Behold, O' Lord, I have endureth my term of iniquity. The almighty one, I truly seek to serve. To endure is not to suffer. The journey for man is to bond with his Lord, God and Jesus Christ. I live for them. They are my rock of salvation. Jesus, my Lord, I trust Your Word, "I am the way, the truth, and the life" (John 14:6). Man must endureth to see the truth and the way.[6]

5. From Kenneth Hagin Jr., "Getting to Know Your Teacher" (message on cassette).

6. "Man Endureth" was inspired by three sources: the book of Job, the teachings on cassette of Reverend Kenneth E. Hagin, and those of his son,

The book of Job became a symbol for me to get well. Job suffered plenty, for he lost his house, children, and livestock, and sustained painful boils (see Job 1:13–19; 2:7–8). Furthermore, within the blink of an eye, Job's life became sheer turmoil. Nevertheless, he persevered through physical, mental, and spiritual adversity, and as a result received healing and blessings from God despite the aforementioned hardships (see Job 42:10–17). Finally, this journal entry clearly foreshadowed God's plan for writing this book. I wrote:

> Praise the Lord! I am alive and therefore must tell my story, awaken or reawaken minds, strengthen people's faith, and spread the gospel to people. I know in my heart that Jesus is coming back one day. Only the father knows this divinely appointed time. I praised Jesus and learned to abide and follow his teachings because he is my mighty counselor, Savior, and the prince of peace. Although this fight has been the toughest event in my life, I have kept the faith during this time of recovery.

ANTIDOTE FOR ADVERSITY

During this process, I had to deal with my head injury while also dealing with Todd's traumatic brain injury. Could you imagine how these accidents made both of our parents feel? To have two sons both head-injured at the same time was overwhelming for me and my family. I learned through reading the Bible not to be anxious because of my situation. You might be thinking, "What am I supposed to be doing if I am not anxious?" My older brother, Todd, was severely head-injured, and I lay in a rehabilitation facility with a traumatic brain injury. Our weakened, depraved human condition ruminates on the pain, stress, and discomfort. How can I not be filled with fear, worry, and anxiety? The solution was my faith in God and his Word, for Scripture clearly states, "Be anxious for nothing, but in everything by prayer and supplication, with thanksgiving, let your requests be made known to God" (Phil 4:6). As I began to pray and ask God for healing of my severe concussion and

Reverend Kenneth Hagin Jr. See Hagin Jr., *Rhema Favorites.*

injured ankle, I found myself thanking God for both blessings and trials in my life. The key word in this verse is *thanksgiving*. Having gratitude instilled an inner peace that fostered physical and emotional healing throughout my body. I counted my blessings rather than focusing on the bruises. Believing God's Word from Philippians 4:6 produced a deep inner peace within my spirit, soul, and body, while the peace of God which surpasses all understanding guarded my heart and mind through Christ Jesus (v. 7).

Throughout my recovery from this tragic accident, my faith continued to be sustained through prayer and study of the Word of God. I learned from this experience to praise the Lord, and to praise God for who he is and what he has done in my life. Although head-injured, I found myself praising God with a joy that resonated from my heart. A journal entry captures this experiential praise of the moment:

I Can't Stop Praising God

I love my precious, sweet God, he is alive, living, and breathing in me. I love Christ. May I do all things through Christ who strengthens me (see Phil 4:13). Yes, yes, oh my precious Christ and Father who diligently watches over me. I praise Your glorious name forever. My belief and faith in Jesus Christ are well intact. The power of God has brought me this far. My faith and belief in Christ has literally saved me. I am alive and healing. Christ is real in me, within my heart and soul because he is for me and is also available to those who believe.

As my faith grew during my recovery time at the rehabilitation facility, I continued to read the Bible and pray to the Lord. When the body and the mind become traumatized, the human spirit can experience a deep, abiding peace. I learned from the psalmist, "Be still, and know that I *am* God; I will be exalted among the nations, I will be exalted in the earth!" (Ps 46:10). Although physically injured, my spirit drew strength from the Word of God. And I took Joshua's directive in the Old Testament, meditating on the Word of God to triumph over physical and emotional adversity. Moses' successor Joshua writes, "This Book of the Law shall not depart from your mouth, but you shall meditate in it day and night, that you may observe to do according to all that is written in it. For then you will make your way prosperous, and then you will have good success" (Josh 1:8).[7]

DIVINE ANALGESIC[8]

I received a lot of pain medication for my shattered leg while in the intensive care unit at the hospital. After the staples were removed from my ankle, I relied upon medicine prescribed by God.[9] My Father in heaven already wrote out a prescription for me and everyone who is a believer in God and his Son, Jesus Christ. And the best part is that this prescription has unlimited refills. Solomon, with all of his wisdom, exhorts believers to put God's Word first in our lives. He writes:

> My son, give attention to my words;
> Incline your ear to my sayings.
> Do not let them depart from your eyes;
> Keep them in the midst of your heart;
> For they *are* life to those who find them,
> And health to all their flesh. (Prov 4:20–22)[10]

I learned that God's Word is available during times of sickness[11] and that he is interested in sustaining and preserving our lives. Deuteronomy 8:3 states, "So He humbled you, allowed you to hunger, and fed you with manna which you did not know nor did your fathers know, that He might make you know that man shall not live by bread alone; but man lives by every *word* that proceeds from the mouth of the LORD." I have learned that while food sustains

7. Joshua 1:8 was brought to my attention from the teachings on cassette of Reverend Kenneth E. Hagin. See Rhema/Kenneth Hagin Ministries at rhema.org.

8. See Hagin, *God's Medicine*.

9. see Hagin, *God's Medicine*.

10. This section from Proverbs 4:20–22 was inspired from the teachings on cassette of Reverend Kenneth E. Hagin. See Rhema/Kenneth Hagin Ministries at rhema.org.

11. See Hagin, *God's Medicine*.

the human body, the Word of God preserves and nourishes the human spirit.[12] As memory about the details before the accident slowly
returned to consciousness, I remembered jogging and listening
to my Walkman when I was hit by the automobile. I learned that
I wasn't paying attention while running with the traffic. The Lord
reminded me that I am a new creation in Christ. My mistakes and
accidents, which God called sins, were forgiven. It is worth repeating
this epistolary promise from the journal entry in the rehabilitation
facility because 2 Corinthians 5:17–19 represents the inspiration of
the Holy Spirit speaking through the apostle Paul. He writes:

> Therefore, if anyone *is* in Christ, *he is* a new creation; old
> things have passed away; behold, all things have become
> new. Now all things *are* of God, who has reconciled us
> to Himself through Jesus Christ, and has given us the
> ministry of reconciliation, that is, that God was in Christ
> reconciling the world to Himself, not imputing their
> trespasses to them, and has committed to us the word of
> reconciliation.

God was telling me that my sins in life, particularly the mistake of
not paying attention while jogging and not running against traffic,
were forgiven. If God wasn't going to remember my sins, then there
wasn't any reason for me to remember them either. All the mistakes
I had ever made in life were now forgiven. My rap sheet was long
and dated back in my life to being a selfish, screaming child. The
material possessions like the boom box, expensive clothes, jewelry,
cars, and vacations were not capable of filling the void in my heart.
I learned from this passage from the Pauline literature that God
forgave me. Moreover, 2 Corintians 5:17–19 provided me with the
reassurance about being a new creation in Christ, for it was God in
Christ who came to the world to be a substitute for my sins and for
your sins. I was healed by God, restored back to life, and learned
that accepting Jesus Christ and becoming a Christian never meant
that life would be devoid of difficulty. Human beings aren't immune
to the furnace of affliction. Hence the sixteen words by the psalmist

12. This section was inspired by the teachings on cassette of Reverend Kenneth E. Hagin. See especially Hagin, *God's Medicine*.

indeed provide encouragement for God's people: "Many *are* the af-flictions of the righteous, But the Lord delivers him out of them all" (Ps 34:19). I had been running from God my whole life and had unsuccessfully attempted to fill the void in my heart with food, alcohol, tobacco, material possessions, education, and the tangible things in life. I was literally running from having a relationship with God. Hence this Old Testament reminder: "For the eyes of the Lord run to and fro throughout the whole earth, to show Himself strong on behalf of *those* whose heart is loyal to Him" (2 Chr 16:9a). This Jewish man from Queens, New York, was saved from death on that road in Fort Lauderdale, Florida. I ran, but couldn't hide from the living God.

LESSON IN ACTION

Whatever you are going through in life, you are not alone. For the psalmist writes, "Call upon Me in the day of trouble; I will deliver you, and you shall glorify Me" (Ps 50:15). Are you hurting physically, emotionally or spiritually right now? If you are, God promises to hear you. Please remember Paul's words, "whoever calls on the name of the Lord shall be saved" (Rom 10:13; see Joel 2:32). Will you call to him?

7

The Walk of Faith

"The thief does not come except to steal, and to kill, and to
destroy. I have come that they may have life, and that they
may have *it* more abundantly."

—JOHN 10:10

A man of integrity, with a clear conscience, can face the
enemy without fear.

—WARREN WIERSBE[1]

FEARFULLY DETERMINED

After a month convalescing at the rehabilitation facility, I returned
home to be with my dad and his wife in South Florida. Arriving
home on crutches, my brain still felt cloudy from the severe concussion. During this time of rehabilitation at home, my father and a
family member drove me to physical therapy a couple of times per

1. In Wiersbe, *Bible Exposition Commentary: New Testament*, vol. 2, p. 58,
under the section "The Equipment (6:13–17)."

week. My physical therapist instructed me to perform exercises at home to strengthen the calf muscles and I was fitted with a boot which went over my fiberglass cast. Both the orthopedist and the physical therapist gave me instructions to walk around with the boot on the left ankle several times during the day. I recall convalescing at home and spending a lot of time lying in bed. I was paralyzed with fear, had painful memories from the accident, and succumbed to this fear by staying on the bed, and rarely arose unless I needed nourishment or had to use the bathroom. My father said to me, "Gregg, you better start walking around or else you will never be able to walk again." Although my father was brusque, deep down those words exemplified "tough love," increasing my fear of not being able to walk. Nevertheless, I knew, as a believer in Jesus Christ, that if I was going to walk it was not going to be on my strength.

SPIRITUAL WARFARE

My father and his wife took a well-needed vacation out of town. My father's wife arranged for her brother-in-law to check on me regularly. He and the housekeeper drove me to the weekly physical therapy appointments. While lying on the bed, I felt impressed by God to walk. As I grabbed the crutches and prepared to walk, I could hear the inner voice saying, "Why are you trying to walk? You can't do this now." I was consumed with doubt and fear. The god of this world, Satan (see 2 Cor 4:4), attempted to destroy God's blessings for my life, as this came in the guise of fear, guilt, doubt, and worry. As I grabbed the crutches to walk one late morning, Satan inflicted doubtful thoughts and this alerted me to remember God's Word which was stored in my heart. David said:

> Your word I have hidden in my heart,
> That I might not sin against You. (Ps 119:11)

It is worth repeating, I recalled in my spirit this verse from the Bible: "You are of God, little children, and have overcome them, because He who is in you is greater than he who is in the world"

(1 John 4:4). I arose from the bed with my crutches and the Word of God in my heart. I was under spiritual attack from Satan and it would be the Word of God that would extinguish the thoughts and feelings of doubt from Satan. I was experiencing my first attack of spiritual warfare and grabbed the shield of faith, which quenches the fiery darts of the wicked one (see Eph 6:16).[2] I made it to the living room area, which was a spacious room with ornate marble floors. As I went through the walking motion, I felt the presence of God and began to recite aloud, "I can do all things through Christ who strengthens me, and I am more than a conqueror through Him who loves me" (see Phil 4:13; Rom 8:37). I slowly made my way into the kitchen and used the digital clock on the microwave to time myself walking. Finally, I walked several times around the house for fifteen minutes and learned to eradicate negative thoughts by speaking the Word of God, a dominant yet indispensable resource for arresting spiritual warfare. The writer of Hebrews explains:

> For the word of God *is* living and powerful, and sharper than any two-edged sword, piercing even to the division of soul and spirit, and of joints and marrow, and is a discerner of the thoughts and intents of the heart. (Heb 4:12)

SERVANT'S HEART

That morning, I had taken a walk of faith that required reliance on God's Word. This walk of faith not only helped me to graduate from the crutches to the cane, but represented a spiritual principle in operation, notably the scriptural lesson of walking by faith and not by sight (see 2 Cor 5:7). This would be a lesson that I would draw upon later in my walk with the Lord. I was healed and restored through faith in God's Word. I began a successful recruiting career and faithfully attended a non-denominational church in South Florida. I served in lay ministry, faithfully attended church services regularly, and met like-minded believers who became dear friends.

---

2. I am indebted to the cassette teachings on spiritual warfare by the late Reverend Kenneth E. Hagin. See Rhema/Kenneth Hagin Ministries at rhema.org.

As a believer in Jesus Christ, I learned to serve the community. With that said, having a servant's heart, I volunteered with my church's convalescent ministry every week at a nursing home in South Florida. The minister preached a church service to the residents at the nursing home. This lay ministry position required visiting the nursing home residents in their rooms and asking if they wanted to attend the worship service. The pastor was a wonderful preacher and human being. At the close of the service, he told the residents, "Now we are going to sing about Jesus." He always had his small children with him at the nursing home service every Sunday. As he hit the first note on his acoustic guitar, his children stood by his side and began to sing, "Jesus loves me this I know, for the Bible tells me so." Jesus Christ spoke about having the heart of a child when confessing sins to God. The bottom line is that children are precious to Jesus! I recalled thinking about how precious children are to the Lord. Jesus said, "Assuredly, I say to you, unless you are converted and become as little children, you will by no means enter the kingdom of heaven . . ." (Matt 18:3). God blessed me immeasurably as I faithfully served these infirm nursing home residents each week. One brother who worked alongside me at the nursing home was a middle-aged man with a heart for the seniors. As I made my rounds to the residents' rooms before the church service, in the corridor there were a multitude of seniors sitting in wheelchairs. This brother grabbed one wheelchair in his left hand and another one in his right hand and wheeled the seniors down the corridor to the church service.

MOMENTS OF CONTEMPLATION

I was serving God, my church, and the community, and wondered where this was leading to in life. I wanted to serve in the ministry and receive training at seminary. I soon learned that God rewards faithful service with more service (see Luke 16:10). I applied for graduate school at Dallas Theological Seminary during the summer of 1997. My pastor from the singles ministry, a friend, and a former university professor wrote letters of recommendation. I had less than a month remaining on the lease of my apartment. Upon receiving an acceptance letter to Dallas Theological Seminary, there was uncertainty about living accommodations in Dallas, for this required prayer to the Lord.

After extensive prayer and apartment research, I submitted an application for a student internship at a residential senior facility in the Dallas–Fort Worth metroplex. They would provide room and board for working part-time at their front desk in the evenings. I recall leaving several voicemail messages for the administrator. During this time, several days remained before my lease was to expire on my apartment in Fort Lauderdale, Florida. At the time, I was selling voicemail services and one afternoon my pager alerted me to a message from the administrator. He said that he met with the executive board and that I was approved to participate in the student internship program. This administrator requested that I type him a letter outlining my graduate work and goals at the seminary. My prayers had been answered. God foreknew my need before I even had the need. Paul writes, "And my God shall supply all your need according to His riches in glory by Christ Jesus" (Phil 4:19).

EXODUS TO TEXAS

Before leaving for Dallas, Texas, I traveled home to see my mother and brother, Todd. He lived several hours north of Queens, New York, and was transported to our house for dinner. When I flew back home to Florida, my friend from church who lived in Fort Lauderdale allowed me to stay at his apartment before my departure to Dallas. My church helped pack up my apartment and received much of the furniture for their Christ-centered halfway house. After staying a month at my friend's apartment, I was ready to depart for Dallas on a Saturday morning, and met two friends at the storage facility on April 19, 1998. The facility stored all of the belongings that I would be taking to Dallas. My two friends helped load all of my belongings onto the trailer that was attached to my automobile.

My travels took me through Florida, Mobile, Alabama, Louisiana, and East Texas. The drive took close to four days and was around fifteen hundred land miles. As I departed Fort Lauderdale, I vividly recall driving north on I-95 towards Orlando, Florida, and during the trip I listened to Christian praise and worship music. As the music played and my heart worshipped God, the recognition of leaving behind a great church and friends caused tears to slowly roll down my cheeks, while my 1997 Ford Escort propelled down the highway towards Dallas, Texas. As a result of my obedience to God, my faithful service of serving seniors was rewarded with more service. God had a ministry for me at the senior facility in the Lone Star State and foreknew my appreciation for senior adults. I began to see God working through many past experiences with older adults and seniors throughout the years. The kindness that I received from my two past counselors and my servant's heart to help my neighbor at the university led to God placing the desire on my heart to serve at the convalescent ministry.

A family photograph that was taken at my mother's apartment in Queens, New York, April 1998. I departed from Fort Lauderdale, Florida, to Dallas, Texas, a few weeks later.

My brother, Todd, and I at our mother's apartment in Queens, New York, 1998.

TIMES OF SERVANTHOOD

I arrived at the senior facility on April 23, 1998 and unloaded my belongings into their small studio apartment. Soon after my arrival at the senior facility, I secured full-time employment at a market research firm that employed many of the Dallas Theological Seminary students. In the evenings, for the rest of the spring and the summer, I worked at the front desk of the retirement facility, checking in family members and spending time talking with the residents. I recall a woman who had just lost her husband, was suffering from an illness, and whose family sent her to the facility for skilled nursing care. She used to visit the front desk and poured her heart out to me. She lamented how she missed her husband. As my heart broke for this widowed woman, I let her vent and provided a caring heart. I soon learned that ministry isn't always about getting up and preaching God's Word. I think it is fair to say that outside the four walls of the church lies a hurting world. What a sad truth! God taught me that ministry was extending his love to others through listening and caring. This was accomplished by keeping my ears and heart open, while keeping my mouth closed. The latter enabled me to minister to this grieving, widowed woman during the evening shift. A short time later that summer, I was asked to lead chapel services at the facility and found myself preaching the Word of God to the seniors on Sunday mornings.

The late-night shifts at the front desk were quiet and there was one resident in particular who always sat on the couch in the living area. He always slept and I discerned the peace of God, especially during the evening shift, for this man's presence on the couch comforted me. Although asleep, he was a familiar face to me as I adjusted to life working at the retirement facility. Next door to my apartment was the locked unit for the Alzheimer's patients. I felt the Spirit of God impressing me to visit this unit. I didn't know why, however, I yielded to the Spirit. If I would have doubted this leading, ultimately I would have talked myself right out of going. The residents in the Alzheimer's unit were unlike the residents at the nursing home in South Florida. These neurologically dazed and incoherent senior adults clearly demonstrated behavior and bodily language signaling that their lights were on but, sadly, nobody was home. They staggered around the unit with their walkers. I attempted to talk to one woman. She said that she was in pain with her back. I laid my hands on her back and started to pray silently to the Lord.

Seminary classes began in late August and I worked part-time at the retirement facility and the market research firm, while pursuing four graduate classes. The senior facility had another student intern and we spent quality time talking about seminary studies and life at this place. One afternoon, I told my friend about being overloaded with work and school. He recommended that I drop a course to accommodate my schedule. Withdrawing from one course made life easier for me with work and the rest of the courses at seminary. The administrator called me into his office and informed me that, due to budgetary reasons, my apartment would be needed to rent. With a thirty-day notice, I began looking around the Dallas area for housing.

One afternoon, my seminary buddy bought me lunch on his meal card in the cafeteria at the seminary. He prayed for me and stood by my side during the housing crisis. He mentioned that I should look in the housing office as there were people who rented rooms to the seminary students. Upon learning this information, I found a man in the east Dallas area who rented rooms to seminary students. This man was an answer to prayer for housing. As I packed my belongings to leave the senior facility, the administrator called me to his office and with a tone of encouragement remarked, "Well, we got you down here." God brought me over fifteen hundred land miles to pray and comfort infirm, lonely senior adults. And he heard my prayers concerning my housing situation. Psalm 145:9 states:

> The LORD *is* good to all,
> And His tender mercies *are* over all His works.

I once heard a pastor state, "If you can take one thing from the pulpit, and apply it to your life, then you will be blessed." I learned a poignant lesson from my time at the retirement facility. It is worth repeating, I relied on God's Word to survive, while focusing on his promises, and never allowed them to depart from my eyes and heart (see Prov 4:20–22). And I knew deep down in my spirit that God would take care of me wherever I went in Dallas, or in the world, for he would always be with me (see Josh 1:9). My sales career and life were progressing nicely until an unexpected crossroads brought me to abysmal depths.

LESSON IN ACTION

It is important to note that the human condition abhors change. If you are preparing for a life transition, and are experiencing uncertainty, fear, and inner turmoil, take hold of God's promise and remember:

> In God I have put my trust;
> I will not be afraid.
> What can man do to me? (Ps 56:11)

8

The Perfect Hit

Finally, my brethren, be strong in the Lord and in the power
of His might.
—EPH 6:10

ROAD OF AFFLICTION

After leaving the senior facility, I completed the semester in the
Christian education program at Dallas Theological Seminary. After
prayerful consideration, I discerned that seminary training wasn't
right to pursue at this time of my life. With that said, this decision
was based on not having a church home or, for that matter, social
and financial stability. Therefore, I needed to move forward to make
a life for myself in Dallas, Texas. After finishing a successful, high-
tech recruiting career, I transitioned to business-to-business sales
and worked for one of the largest independent yellow-page books
in North Texas. After the yellow-page company was acquired, I left
them to sell newspaper advertising for a community newspaper

and, ultimately, secured an account executive position for a company specializing in sensory marketing.

It was an early fall morning on November 3, 2011, and I was preparing to travel to my office for a sales meeting with the district sales manager and the sales team. I proceeded to drive from my home towards Beltline Road, the intersection each day that took me to the freeway. I approached the stop sign, looked to the left and saw traffic approaching, and then proceeded to cross over to the other side of Beltline Road. While driving across Beltline Road, I took my eyes off of the oncoming traffic on the left side and quickly shifted my attention to the oncoming traffic on the right side of the road. I looked to my left side and observed a black car coming fast towards the passenger door. A second elapsed, and within the blink of an eye I sustained the hardest hit that I had ever experienced in my life! Within a few seconds of the impact, my Honda Accord spun around straight, while my foot gunned the accelerator with sheer intensity.

Realizing what happened, I stopped the car about forty yards down the road. Feeling shaken, I grabbed the work cell phone, called my wife, and told her about the car accident. She said emphatically, "I am on my way. I will be there in a little bit." I immediately called 911 and informed the dispatcher about being in an automobile accident. After a cell phone conversation with my district sales manager, I heard the piercing sounds of the ambulance sirens closing in on the accident scene. I reached over to open the driver's-side door and it wouldn't open. The paramedic entered the automobile through the passenger's-side window and proceeded to take my blood pressure. I was filled with fear as the paramedic questioned me about being able to walk. Moreover, there was a strange tingling sensation on the left side of my head. Shortly thereafter, my wife, Valerie, arrived, came into the passenger's seat, hugged me, and said, "It is going to be okay."

After completing the police report, I felt calmer and managed to drive the car to my house. After the insurance company was notified, I filed a claim and immediately took the car to my trusted auto body mechanic. I came to the realization later in the afternoon that I had been functioning on pure adrenalin. As these effects minimized, I felt tired, dizzy, and nauseous, therefore my wife took me to the emergency room, where a CT scan was performed on my skull. The scan was normal and I was sent home with pain medication, while the physician informed me that I had sustained a concussion. Consequentially the neurological symptoms from this car accident caused dizziness and a headache which kept me up for most of the night following the hospital visit.

NEUROLOGICAL OVERLOAD

The next day, my wife, Valerie, had the day off from work and I accompanied her to run errands in the community. I recall becoming ill with motion sickness from the car ride, and upon arriving at home she helped me out of the car, when I became frozen in a catatonic state. Unable to walk or move, there was a delayed reaction of the neurons firing in my brain. Therefore, I took small steps with the assistance from my wife and experienced difficulty talking and organizing my thoughts into speech. Several days transpired and the headaches intensified. I was advised by a family friend to obtain a second opinion from another hospital in Dallas. Valerie arrived home from work and stated that she was taking me to a different hospital.

We arrived at the emergency room around 5 p.m. As I waited for medical treatment, the movement of the room felt like slow-motion frames transcending the ephemeral beat of time, while intensifying the neurological symptoms of the concussion. With that said, fear consumed every mortal fiber of my being. Eventually, the nurse escorted me into the treatment room, took vital signs, and reported a blood pressure reading of 178/105. The possibility of dying at this hospital became a fearful realization to me. Therefore, I recall feeling as though my wife, Valerie, would be seeing me for the last time. I was escorted back to the waiting room area until a bed became available. After receiving medical treatment, I was diagnosed with a concussion, given a mild sedative, and counseled by the medical personnel to rest at home.

Days had passed since the car accident; the headaches and the dizziness persisted, while insomnia and depression consumed my being with intensity. I was referred to a neurologist by one of our friends from Sunday school and soon learned the reasons behind my debilitating neurological symptoms of, headaches, dizziness, difficulty concentrating, short-term memory issues, sensitivity to noise, insomnia, talking and walking issues, and depression. During the medical examination, I told the neurologist about my symptoms and with lucid candor he exclaimed, "You definitely have post-concussion syndrome." This wise neurologist informed me and my wife that the concussions and head injuries that were sustained throughout my past had become cumulative, causing neurological symptoms from this mild traumatic brain injury. The doctor recited three words and asked me to repeat them back to him. I repeated the words, however, when the neurologist asked me several minutes later to recite these words, I was unable to remember them. When the automobile struck the driver's-side door, the impact caused blunt-force trauma to the side of my head, and this was the reason why I experienced short-term memory loss. The neurological trauma compromised my brain's functional and biochemical integrity, requiring rest and time to heal.

WHEN IN PAIN, PRAY

The healing process was slow and painful. I was on short-term disability from work and lay on the couch day after day trying to heal from this mild traumatic brain injury. Days passed and I began to feel well enough to take a walk outside. I listened to Christian praise and worship music, which facilitated healing from the accident. The air outside was refreshing and prompted me to walk for an hour one afternoon. On this short walk, my cassette player headphones transmitted the Word of God, and as a result I praised and worshipped God with a grateful heart. Moreover, while walking and listening to Christian music, my whole being was filled with thanksgiving and praise, while the thanksgiving occurred first, followed by the praises. The latter and the former are relational, and when combined, elicit comfort and peace. An answer to prayer came when two men from the Sunday school class took me out for dinner. At this point, I was happy to get away from the house. Upon my arrival at the restaurant, I sat down to eat and within minutes the room spun out of control, producing dizziness. This moment of neurological delirium, namely, vertigo, is a common symptom of post-concussion syndrome. I spent the next six weeks after the accident convalescing at home and experienced restlessness and neurological discomfort. At times, my blood pressure was elevated and I experienced the sensation similar to the experience at the emergency room. Furthermore, I had intense headaches, thinking hurt, and I was scared and full of fear. Because I stored God's promises in my heart, I was able to rely on them during a time of intense physical pain and despair. In times of fear, remember these words from the psalmist:

> Whenever I am afraid,
> I will trust in You.
> In God (I will praise His word),
> In God I have put my trust;
> I will not fear.
> What can flesh do to me? (Ps 56:3–4)

THE ART OF MEDITATION

Because I put my trust in God and his Word, I was able to have peace of mind. While meditating on Scripture during a time of neurological and emotional distress, God's Word spoke to my spirit, just like he did back in 1992 while convalescing at the re-habilitation facility. As I meditated on those wonderful promises from David, my breathing slowed and the tingling in my fingers subsided. God's Word comforted me, while prayer greatly reduced the pain from the intense headaches. Lying still, I meditated on the Word of God and learned through Bible study to immerse my mind and spirit in the Pauline literature. The epistolary letters had been a source of comfort nineteen years ago when I was recovering from the traumatic brain injury. I meditated on the Word of God while recovering from this recent mild traumatic brain injury by repeat-ing Scripture in my heart. Furthermore, I realigned my thinking to

God's thoughts and his Word, therefore this relieved my discouraged heart and produced a feeling of well-being. Simply put, when we recognize that God's thoughts supersede our thought life, it is then and only then when we surrender our mind to the Lord. The prophet Isaiah declared:

> "For My thoughts *are* not your thoughts,
> Nor *are* your ways My ways," says the LORD.
> "For *as* the heavens are higher than the earth,
> So are My ways higher than your ways,
> And My thoughts than your thoughts." (Isa 55:8–9)

BELIEVING GOD'S WORD

My in-laws, Fred and Joy Allen, celebrated their fifty-third wedding anniversary several years ago. My wife and her three brothers made arrangements for the celebration party at their church in Fort Worth, Texas. I recall greeting family members and friends of my in-laws at this celebration event. As the vertigo returned with intense fervor, I excused myself from the party, entered the church sanctuary, and lay down on the pew. With tears rolling down my cheeks, I prayed to God for the dizziness and the vertigo to subside. As I cried silently and prayed, there was deep communion while praying and talking to God. I recalled a verse of Scripture that ministered to me after the traumatic brain injury in 1992, namely, Mark 11:24, where Jesus states, "Therefore I say to you, whatever things you ask when you pray, believe that you receive *them,* and you will have *them.*" I desired healing from the dizziness, therefore I believed in my heart that I was well even though my injured brain said otherwise.[1] I returned back to the neurologist a few times after this car accident. At the third visit, my blood pressure was a healthy 121/75, the vertigo dissipated, and I was healed from the agonizing

---

1. Mark 11:23–24 were the two Synoptic Gospel verses that facilitated healing for Reverend Kenneth E. Hagin. I recalled his testimony of healing, while lying on the church pew. See Hagin, "My Testimony of Healing" (message on cassette).

symptoms of post-concussion syndrome. My Lord fulfilled his promise in Scripture. Christ teaches:

> If you abide in Me, and My words abide in you, you will
> ask what you desire, and it shall be done for you. By this
> My Father is glorified, that you bear much fruit; so you
> will be My disciples. (John 15:7–8)

I believed for healing and the Lord made this a reality in my life because I am a *talmid* of *Yeshua* (Heb., disciple of Jesus). The hit that I sustained from that oncoming car should have seriously injured or killed me. Moreover, my Honda Accord could have been tossed into oncoming traffic or spun out of control. However, none of these things occurred, as he was in control of the situation. For God foreknew the consequences of this mistake and equipped me with faith to endure another neurological trauma. The best medicine is God's Word![2] There was, indeed, a miracle that day on November 3, 2011. Because I believed in Jesus Christ, and the Holy Spirit lived within my spirit, God enabled me to survive a near-fatal car accident, which produced a healing from the Lord.

LESSON IN ACTION

It is during the most painful times in our lives when God is closer than we could ever imagine. If you are in physical, emotional, or spiritual pain right now, and are not sure what to do, may the psalmist's words comfort your soul:

> Be merciful to me, O God, be merciful to me!
> For my soul trusts in You;
> And in the shadow of Your wings I will make my refuge,
> Until *these* calamities have passed by. (Ps 57:1)

---

2. See Hagin, *God's Medicine.*

9

Saved, Not by Accident

For the wages of sin *is* death, but the gift of God *is* eternal life
in Christ Jesus our Lord.

—ROM 6:23

MEDICINE FOR THE SOUL

It is my prayer that as you read the following material your faith
will be enriched in the Lord. If you are unsure of God and how to
receive eternal life, then the following sentences will be a blessing
to you. I received from God because of an open heart, mind, and
spirit. If someone had told me that I would become a born-again
believer in Jesus Christ, I would have told them they were *meshug-
gener* (Yiddish, crazy). No one beat me over the head with the Bible.
I was led by the Spirit of God. The prophet Zechariah declares:

> So he answered and said to me:
>
> "This *is* the word of the LORD to Zerubbabel:
> 'Not by might nor by power, but by My Spirit,'
> Says the LORD of hosts." (Zech 4:6)

Let me guide you through this process. First, God sent his Son, Jesus Christ, into the world for several reasons. John writes, "In the beginning was the Word, and the Word was with God, and the Word was God. He was in the beginning with God. All things were made through Him, and without Him nothing was made that was made" (John 1:1–3). Jesus Christ was born of a virgin named Mary, and before his birth the angel of the Lord appeared to shepherds while they were watching their flock during the evening. Luke writes:

> Then the angel said to them, "Do not be afraid, for behold, I bring you good tidings of great joy which will be to all people. For there is born to you this day in the city of David a Savior, who is Christ the Lord. And this *will be* the sign to you: You will find a Babe wrapped in swaddling clothes, lying in a manger." (Luke 2:10–12)

Second, Jesus Christ was called by God to hang on the cross and endure a painful, agonizing death. Jesus loved you and me so much that he went to the cross to die for our sins. Paul writes, "But God demonstrates His own love towards us, in that while we were still sinners, Christ died for us" (Rom 5:8). In the Old Testament, (Heb., *Tanakh*, the Hebrew Scriptures) the priests entered the holy of holies and sacrificed the life of the animals for the sins of man. We read in the book of Leviticus how blood is representative of life:

> 'And whatever man of the house of Israel, or of the strangers who dwell among you, who eats any blood, I will set My face against that person who eats blood, and will cut him off from among his people. For the life of the flesh *is* in the blood, and I have given it to you upon the altar to make atonement for your souls; for it *is* the blood *that* makes atonement for the soul.' (Lev 17:10–11)

Thank God today, via the Messiah's blood-atoning sacrifice, we don't have to shed the blood of animals for the remission of sins. As Christ hung from the cross, the shedding of his blood consummated the beginning of the New Testament. And this New Covenant in which we live in today has been sanctified by the precious blood of Jesus Christ. In God's great plan of redemption, he sent his son to share the gospel, which literally means "good news." For God foreknew that we needed a Savior, friend, and comforter in this life. When Jesus was preparing to go to the cross, he instructed the disciples that he was leaving to die. However, he would send the Holy Spirit as a comforter after he ascended from the cross to be with the Father in heaven. Jesus infused hope within the disciples, promising them a greater blessing after his departure. He stated, "Nevertheless I tell you the truth. It is to your advantage that I go away; for if I do not go away, the Helper will not come to you; but if I depart, I will send Him to you" (John 16:7).

After Jesus took his last breath on the cross and died, on the third day he arose from the grave victorious over death. As pastor Dr. Charles L. Wilson passionately proclaims, "The resurrection changed everything!" Amen! Those words have changed my life and they have set the stage for our eternity. In John's Gospel, a time-less message for humanity, John the Baptist ties the Hebrew Scriptures together with the New Testament, for he proclaims thirteen profound words that confirm and remind you, me, and the world who Jesus was and why he came to the earth. John writes, "Behold! The Lamb of God who takes away the sin of the world!" (John 1:29).

WHAT HAPPENS WHEN YOU DIE?

At some point in life, you will think about death, for this time of questioning represents a critical juncture on your journey of life. I would like to ask you three questions, and all I ask of you is to be honest with yourself and God. Have you ever wondered where you will go after you die? Second, listen to the words from the late Dr. D. James Kennedy: "Have you come to a place in your spiritual life where you know for certain that if you were to die today you would go to heaven, or is that something you would say you're still working on?"[1] Finally, have you ever made mistakes in your life? Perhaps you succumbed to a temptation that caused harm to you or other people. An unwise decision may have cost you a job, a re-lationship, and your peace of mind. You may have been involved

1. Kennedy, *Evangelism Explosion*, 31, under "E. Two diagnostic questions."

in an automobile accident where you were at fault. You may have been the victim of a car accident, or you may have received a discouraging diagnosis from the doctor. Maybe you just lost your job after you served your company faithfully for years, even decades. Perhaps right now your loved one is ill in the hospital. There may be heartache from the death or loss of a loved one. You may be enduring physical or emotional pain from a sickness or an injury.

Perhaps right now you or a family member have sustained serious trauma, such as a traumatic brain injury or a spinal cord injury. Whatever the issue, you can rest assured that God loves you and wants to come into your life as Savior, friend, and comforter. I want to ask you another question. Do you think that God is mad at you for something that you have done to yourself or to someone in your life? The prophet Jeremiah declared that God loves you with an everlasting love (see Jer 31:3). Therefore, God isn't mad at you; he is madly in love with you! Second, it is worth repeating from chapter 6, there isn't anything that you can do to earn your way into heaven! Paul teaches, "For by grace you have been saved through faith, and that not of yourselves; *it is* the gift of God, not of works, lest anyone should boast" (Eph 2:8–9). I came to the realization in life that money, job status, education, material possessions, and worldly items couldn't fill the void in my heart or promise entrance into heaven. God wants to have an honest, transparent, and meaningful relationship with you. The best thing is that you can come just as you are. God will accept you right where you are in your life. With your head bowed and eyes closed, pray the following words sincerely from your heart:

> Father in heaven, I come to you in the name of Jesus Christ. He says, "All that the Father gives Me will come to Me, and the one who comes to Me I will by no means cast out" (John 6:37).[2] I come to you knowing that you will not cast me away, but take me in. God, I am a sinner and have fallen short of the glory of God (see Rom 3:23). I repent of my sins and place my faith and trust

---

2. John 6:37 and the accompanying phrase is from my memory of the Sinner's Prayer which I prayed to receive the Lord, as found in a 1992 issue of *The Word of Faith* monthly magazine.

in Christ for these sins. Please come into my life to be my Savior and friend. I confess with my mouth the Lord Jesus and believe in my heart that God raised him from the dead (Rom 10:9). I believe this in my heart, and with my mouth I make my confession to you for salvation (see Rom 10:10). If I were to die today, your Word promises me that to be absent from the body is to be present with you, the risen Lord (see 2 Cor 5:8). I am now saved. Thank You God for saving me and forgiving me from my sins. Amen.

NEW LIFE IN CHRIST

Welcome to the kingdom of God! If you prayed this prayer of salvation, I rejoice with you and say, "*Mazel tov*" (congratulations). You have made the most significant decision of your life. I encourage you to join a Bible-believing church. As a new believer in Jesus Christ, you are much like a newborn baby, who requires food in order to grow. The Word of God teaches, "Therefore, laying aside all malice, all deceit, hypocrisy, envy, and all evil speaking, as new born babes, desire the pure milk of the word, that you may grow thereby, if indeed you have tasted that the Lord *is* gracious" (1 Pet 2:1–3). If you are a born-again believer in Jesus Christ, I ask you to pray for the people who may be reading this book who have recited the Sinner's Prayer to receive the Lord. When I began questioning God and Jesus Christ, I wrote a few ministries that I had heard of from the radio and asked many questions about my faith in God through Jesus Christ. Remember James's words, "Confess *your* trespasses to one another, and pray for one another, that you may be healed. The effective, fervent prayer of a righteous man avails much" (Jas 5:16).

FALLEN, BUT NOT FORGOTTEN

Perhaps you are a believer in Jesus Christ but have fallen away from the church. Maybe you are dipping your cup in the wrong well of life. Caffeine maybe your choice of drink because of its taste and ability to jump-start the day. However, its short-lived effect requires more at the expense of sleep. Sugar-free iced tea seems to "hit the spot." However, your body craves something else to gratify your thirst. Soon thereafter, you discover that drinking cold water alleviates your dry palate, satisfying your thirst. Albeit a wise choice for sustenance, Jesus states, "Whoever drinks of this water will thirst again, but whoever drinks of the water that I shall give him will never thirst. But the water that I shall give him will become in him a fountain of water springing up into everlasting life" (John 4:13–14).[3] Hence the true source of water from God's well lies in Jesus Christ.

If you have fallen away from God and this book has spoken to your heart, you may feel led by the Holy Spirit to recommit your life to Christ. In the book of Jeremiah, we experience the picture of people being lost like sheep. They have sinned and become devoured by the world. For you, this could be in the form of guilt, worry, pride, anger, betrayal, envy, lust, poverty, infidelity, unemployment, disease, or illness. The prophet Jeremiah from the Old Testament clearly tells it like it is. He describes this backslidden state:

> "My people have been lost sheep.
> Their shepherds have led them astray;
> They have turned them away *on* the mountains.
> They have gone from mountain to hill;
> They have forgotten their resting place.
> All who have found them have devoured them;
> And their adversaries said, 'We have not offended,
> Because they have sinned against the LORD, the habitation of justice,
> The LORD, the hope of their fathers.'" (Jer 50:6–7)

Can you relate to these statements from Jeremiah? Perhaps you are at a place in your life where it is time to return to God. If you have fallen away from God, with your eyes closed and your heart open to God, repeat this prayer:

> Father in heaven, I have fallen away from you, your Word and your people. Lord Jesus, I am returning to the fold, for I am like a sheep that has gone astray and now return

---

3. This scenario was influenced from a pastor many years ago.

back to the Shepherd, the Overseer of my soul (see 1 Pet
2:25). Forgive me for not walking with you. Right now,
I surrender and submit my life to you. God, your Word
says, "For I know the thoughts that I think toward you,
says the LORD, thoughts of peace and not of evil, to give
you a future and a hope. Then you will call upon Me and
go and pray to Me, and I will listen to you. And you will
seek Me and find *Me,* when you search for Me with all
your heart" (Jer 29:11–13). Thank you God for taking me
back to the Shepherd, Jesus Christ. Amen.

WELCOME BACK

Mazel tov (congratulations) on recommitting your life to the Lord!
This is the beginning of a powerful testimony for you. My pastor
and friend Dr. Charles L. Wilson states, "You can't have a testimony
until you have a test." I trust you will do great things for God because I don't believe in luck or accidents, for God created each and
every one of us for a purpose. Did you know that God knew you
before you were ever conceived? In the Old Testament, the psalmist describes God knowing us even before we were formed in the
womb:

> For You formed my inward parts;
> You covered me in my mother's womb.
> I will praise You, for I am fearfully *and* wonderfully made;
> Marvelous are Your works,
> And *that* my soul knows very well.
> My frame was not hidden from You,
> When I was made in secret,
> *And* skillfully wrought in the lowest parts of the earth.
> Your eyes saw my substance, being yet unformed.
> And in Your book they all were written,
> The days fashioned for me,
> When *as yet there were* none of them.
> (Ps 139:13–16)

If you recited the Sinner's Prayer for the first time or returned
back to the Lord, then this is a wonderful new start for your life!

As you seek the Lord in prayer and fellowship, I encourage you to attend a Bible-believing church. Remember, it is important to consider being with like-minded believers. The book of Hebrews teaches, "And let us consider one another in order to stir up love and good works, not forsaking the assembling of ourselves together, as *is* the manner of some, but exhorting *one another,* and so much the more as you see the Day approaching" (Heb 10:24–25). When attending church, I want to encourage you to get plugged into a Sunday school group. At these groups you will meet people, form friendships, and receive encouragement from Christians who love the Lord. The church is the place to live out your faith with the community of believers. Please pray about how and where God can use you. As you grow in your Christian faith, may your life reflect Christlikeness while ministering to people's deepest need.

LESSON IN ACTION

When we commit our life to the Lord and to his care, we can have confidence that when we die we will go immediately into his presence. He restores our weary soul that has become burdened with the stressors of life. Jesus states:

> Come to Me, all *you* who labor and are heavy laden, and I will give you rest. Take My yoke upon you and learn from Me, for I am gentle and lowly in heart, and you will find rest for your souls. For my yoke *is* easy and My burden is light. (Matt 11:28–30)

10

Encouragement Facilitates Healing

Death and life *are* in the power of the tongue,
And those who love it will eat its fruit.
—PROV 18:21

WORDS ARE SMALL THINGS THAT HOLD INCREDIBLE
POWER.
—ADELE AHLBERG CALHOUN[1]

THE MAGNITUDE OF SPEECH

Kind words emitted from our mouth, whether directed to others or spoken to us by other people, can be like water to a parched, dehydrated being. Soothing words comfort a troubled heart, while listening to hateful, derogatory speech from angry, demeaning people hurts and injures others, much like a hand grenade whose shrapnel pierces through the flesh causing irreparable harm to the physical body. In fact, volatile speech toward others fuels discouragement,

---

1. Calhoun, *Spiritual Disciplines Handbook*, 187.

injures the soul, and consequentially fosters psychopathology within the recipient. Dr. Charles L. Wilson, senior pastor of Central Baptist Church, believes that "hurt people, hurt people." What a sad reality! Solomon in all of his wisdom asserted that a person is snared by the words of their mouth (see Prov 6:2). Furthermore, we must never miscalculate the tongue's lethal outcome towards others. R. Kent Hughes warns, "The tongue, so tiny, is immensely powerful."[2] And it reminds us to consider its referential source of origin, namely, that derogatory, unsavory words from people quite frankly emanate to the core of being, the human heart. Christ explains, "For out of the heart proceed evil thoughts, murders, adulteries, fornications, thefts, false witness, blasphemies" (Matt 15:19). With that said, I challenge you with two questions: What kind of words are coming out of your mouth when you are speaking to people? What about the words that you are hearing from other people? Take a moment to close your eyes, quiet your mind, and pray about this matter. If there are memories of inappropriate speech from your mouth, repent and confess this to the Lord. If someone has spoken mean and cruel words to you, simply tell the Lord about it and pray for them.

I want to share a profound experience which occurred several years ago in the workplace. I remember when my boss requested to speak to me in the conference room. This employer yelled at me, hurling profane, insulting words. When I heard this it was like being kicked in the solar plexus and getting the wind knocked out of me. Moments like this help us to understand the bipolar yet unpredictable tendency of the human heart. The Old Testament prophet Jeremiah declared, "The heart is deceitful above all *things*, And desperately wicked; Who can know it?" (Jer 17:9). This employer appeared pleasant, then without warning I saw the depraved, angry, desperate side of the human heart. As the hours and the days passed after leaving this job, I became angry towards this former boss.

2. Hughes, *Disciplines of a Godly Man*, 143.

THE POWER OF FORGIVENESS

The turning point for me came when the interim pastor at Sunnyvale First Baptist Church preached a sermon about prayer and forgiveness from Matthew 6:9–15. On that dismal Sunday morning, my heart was beat to a pulp and felt like it endured a ten-round heavyweight boxing match. Have you ever felt like this? I have encouraging news from a godly, wise pastor. Dr. Barry Creamer preached a deeply profound message, namely, that if we have been hurt by harmful, derogatory words, then if we go to the Lord in prayer we must forgive those who have hurt us if we desire to receive from God. This minister referenced the Words of Jesus Christ, "For if you forgive men their trespasses, your heavenly Father will also forgive you. But if you do not forgive men their trespasses, neither will your Father forgive your trespasses" (vv. 14–15). And because Christ forgave us, we should be compelled to forgive others if a person becomes verbally abusive towards us. Dr. Creamer's message ministered to me in a mighty way. Therefore I learned to forgive this former employer, and it is my hope that you too will learn to forgive others so that you can receive his blessings during times of prayer. Finally, it is imperative to expound upon the lifeblood of human experience, especially the interpersonal enterprise. The bottom line is that human beings need encouragement! Paul's epistolary letter captures the essence of affirming people, while emphasizing salvation in Jesus Christ. He writes:

> For God did not appoint us to wrath, but to obtain salvation through our Lord Jesus Christ, who died for us, that whether we wake or sleep, we should live together with Him. Therefore comfort each other and edify one another, just as you also are doing. (1 Thess 5:9–11)

TRANSMITTING ENCOURAGEMENT

I want to draw your attention to an important visitor at the head injury rehabilitation facility from chapter 6, specifically my father's friend, the minister who spent time with me after the traumatic brain injury. I had survived a near-death experience and my body was recovering from the serious trauma. It is worth repeating, after this minister prayed with me and my parents, he stated, "Gregg, I expect to hear good things from you." My former pastor from the singles ministry in South Florida always encouraged me, stating, "Gregg, I believe in you; you will do great." Pastor Dan exemplifies a Christian role model, for he believed in me and encouraged me in the Lord. These two men personified role models of the Christian faith, mainly in word, deed, and action. Paul writes:

> *Be* kindly affectionate to one another with brotherly love, in honor giving preference to one another; not lagging in diligence, fervent in spirit, serving the Lord; rejoicing in hope, patient in tribulation, continuing steadfastly in prayer; distributing to the needs of the saints, given to hospitality. (Rom 12:10–12)

My friend and brother in the Lord Dr. Charles L. Wilson always exhorted me with encouragement, stating, "Gregg, you are a world-changer for Christ." In 2012, he celebrated twenty-five years of service to the Lord as the senior pastor of Sunnyvale First Baptist Church. He and his wife, Paulette, are "shepherds of vision, service and love!"[3] During Dr. Wilson's sermon on April 22, 2012, we learned to model our lives after the motivation of the apostle Paul, for he was eager and not ashamed of the gospel. Dr. Wilson exemplifies a man who is committed, ready, and obligated to share the gospel to all people. I am grateful that he was my pastor at the time, because he clearly demonstrated a love for God and a love towards his people. Moreover, he has taught me that ministry is encouraging and affirming people. Finally, Dr. Wilson advocates, "The most effective leaders help others to be successful." Are there people in your life that you can help to be successful? If you are helping others, then I rejoice with you. If you are unsure of the aforementioned question, then perhaps this is an opportune moment to pray about helping others to succeed. Does anyone come to mind? Would you commit this right now to prayer? As you seek the Lord in prayer,

3. Sunnyvale First Baptist Church, *Order of Worship*, April 22, 2012, back cover.

ask him to lead you to others in need. Jesus teaches, "Ask, and it will be given to you; seek, and you will find; knock, and it will be opened to you. For everyone who asks receives, and he who seeks finds, and to him who knocks it will be opened" (Matt 7:7–8).

I was in the process of completing the reading for a forthcoming graduate class at Trinity Theological Seminary and felt impressed by the Lord to talk with a man at the coffee house who was sitting behind me, reading intently. As we talked with each other and shared about God, I shared about being a student at seminary and learned that he was a believer in Jesus Christ. As a result, we encouraged each other in the Christian faith. How did I know that he was a Christian? It was not me, for it was the Holy Spirit within who drew me to this brother in Christ.

Once again, it is worth repeating, believers in Jesus Christ must encourage and affirm others in order to make a positive difference in their lives. As we approach the first quarter of the twenty-first century, we remain cognizant about living in a hectic, chaotic world. How many people fail to ask others how their day is going, or how they are doing? When you arrive at the cash register in the grocery store or visit a restaurant, do you encourage the employees? We don't know these people, however, we know from the Word of God: "Therefore, as we have opportunity, let us do *good to all*, especially to those who are of the household of faith" (Gal 6:10, emphasis added).

I recall the terrible wildfires that raged through Northern California. Negative words are much like wildfires that engulf the human soul and the body, for they discourage, hurt, and destroy a person's emotional, physical, and spiritual well-being. Perhaps you heard negative remarks from a loved one while growing up. Let's not tell our spouses, parents, children, friends, or coworkers negative comments. Instead, let's build them up and tell them that they will do great things. In a genuine tone, tell them that you believe in them. If they are a Christian, you can tell them that they can do all things through Christ who gives them strength (see Phil 4:13). Finally, remember that the noblest thing that you can do for people is to listen to them and genuinely care for their lives. Is this something that you need help with? Take a moment right now and ask the

Lord for help with listening and caring. When the Holy Spirit calms your mind and soul from life's preoccupation, the *Jehovah Shalom* (Heb., God of Peace) improves your listening, thus strengthening your empathy towards others in need. For it is then and only then that you can focus intently on others.

BE TRUE TO GOD

My former counselor and professor from Norwich University dedicated his life to teaching and the learning condition of students, while my former pastors Dan Plourde and Dr. Charles L. Wilson have committed their lives to serving the Lord and caring for the spiritual condition of his people. Can you imagine if we all dedicated our lives to God and to his people? If every person demonstrated a genuine, deep concern for other people's lives, then we wouldn't have homeless, hungry, and discouraged people in our communities, cities, and the world. As we draw close to the return of Christ, every person on earth will have to give an account of their life to God. We will have to stand before a holy God and explain how we used the spiritual gifts that he bestowed upon us to bless other people in order to make a positive difference for him in our communities around the world. The writer to the Hebrews explains:

> And as it is appointed for men to die once, but after
> this the judgment, so Christ was offered once to bear
> the sins of many. To those who eagerly wait for Him He
> will appear a second time, apart from sin, for salvation.
> (Heb 9:27–28)

I grew up in a successful, upper-middle-class home and environment. Success was equated with earning a lot of money, receiving a good education, and living a life with material possessions. In the 1980s, as an upper-middle-class Jewish male, the mandate of acquiring material possessions was the expectation and, sadly, the norm. At the country clubs where my father held membership, I recall the affluent lifestyles of the men and the women, while becoming cognizant of their views on life. For example, I specifically remember an older gentleman talking with me while standing in the shallow section of the swimming pool. When I informed this man about being a college student and my desire to pursue the field of counseling and psychology, he remarked, "There isn't any money in that." Growing away from this lifestyle taught me that money can't buy happiness, and as my spiritual life strengthened in the church, godly men and woman taught me to be true to God, true to his Word, and true to his people. Is this something you need to consider? If the latter statement applies to you and requires change, would you commit this to prayer right now? Close your eyes, open your heart, and ask God to help you to be true to him, true to his Word, and true to his people. Ask the Lord to search your heart, while allowing the psalmist's words to penetrate your soul:

> Search me, O God, and know my heart;
> Try me, and know my anxieties;
> And see if *there is any* wicked way in me,
> And lead me in the way everlasting. (Ps 139:23–24)

LIFEBLOOD OF RELATIONSHIPS

My friend from the support group that I attended after my traumatic brain injury in South Florida taught me the value of caring for people. The latter encapsulates the lifeblood of the interpersonal enterprise. For example, Dr. Charles L. Wilson demonstrated concern during my recovery from the mild traumatic brain injury in 2011. He picked me up at my house for lunch and we ate at a local delicatessen in the neighborhood, where he shared about his life experiences in Oklahoma. We laughed and had a wonderful time in the Lord. This fueled my heart with love and healing, for this man of God who co-officiated my wedding and preached the Word of God every Sunday stepped down from the pulpit and sat beside me as a friend. On that day, I experienced the love of God through the Holy Spirit shed abroad from his heart (see Rom 5:5). It is worth repeating, Dr. Charles L. Wilson exemplifies a man who has faithfully served God's people, for this brother's faithful obedience clearly echoes Paul's admonition for pastors. Paul writes, "I, therefore, the prisoner of the Lord, beseech you to walk worthy of the calling with which you were called, with all lowliness and gentleness, with long-suffering, bearing with one another in love, endeavoring to keep the unity of the Spirit in the bond of peace" (Eph 4:1–3).

My former pastor has lived out an authentic, humble life before his people, teaching me the value of serving others. Parrett and Kang remind us, "Humility, then, is something we *do*. Only in the doing are we blessed. Only in the doing are we following the example of our humble Lord. As we give ourselves to God and neighbor in these ways, God cultivates within us the virtue of true humility."[4] The Sunday school book entitled *Miracles: The Transforming Power of Jesus* (*A Study of Matthew*) illustrates a compelling lesson by Charles Glidewell from Matthew 15:21–28,[5] elucidating the functional role of Christian humility. He notes:

> The Christian life is a life of humility. It is a life of constant realignment with God's will. And it is a life characterized by the deep conviction that nothing is impossible with God. Because he is the object of our faith, great faith does not give up.[6]

My friend, all that God requires of you, me, and his people above anything that this world has to offer are three words: *obedience to him*. We must exercise humility towards others in our family, community, place of employment, and throughout this twenty-first-century global sphere. What areas in your life need humility? Take a moment to consider if this is needed with family, coworkers, friends, and others in your life. If you can identify areas in your life requiring improvement with humility, right now, why not close your eyes, open your heart, and ask the Lord for help.

LESSON IN ACTION

Words can either comfort or hurt people. We must never underestimate the power of the tongue, for it contains the power of life

---

4. Parrett and Kang, *Teaching the Faith*, 186.
5. Glidewell, "From Desperation to Faith," 93–100.
6. Glidewell, "From Desperation to Faith," 98–99.

or death (see Jas 3:8–9).[7] Take note of this power in your tongue! And remember, the mark of a godly man or woman is determined when they put others first before themselves. This means not even thinking of yourself at all. When you are around people, consider modeling your life after Jesus Christ, for he exemplified godliness and humility, especially toward others. Take heed to Paul's directive about selflessness. He writes:

> Let nothing *be done* through selfish ambition or conceit, but in lowliness of mind let each esteem others better than himself. Let each of you look out not only for his own interests, but also for the interests of others. (Phil 2:3–4)

7. See Calhoun, *Spiritual Disciplines Handbook*, 186–187.

11

Heavenly Perspectives

For the things which are seen *are* temporary, but the things
which are not seen *are* eternal.
—2 COR 4:18B

REEXAMINED LIFE

I was raised in the synagogue, never had the opportunity to hear
the gospel, and consequentially I didn't have anyone to talk to about
the Bible before coming to faith in the Lord. It is worth repeating, I
wrote a few ministries for spiritual guidance and truly believed that
these ministerial workers were praying for me as I searched for an-
swers in the Bible. Reflecting back to Todd's accident, I can see how
God took a terrible tragedy and used it for his glory, for I cried out
to God and he heard my prayers regarding healing for my brother.
Furthermore, I was led by the Spirit of God. Paul writes, "For as
many as are led by the Spirit of God, these are sons of God" (Rom
8:14). My profession that I believed in the Lord Jesus and that God
raised him from the dead brought me into the kingdom of God.

In addition to a personal relationship with Jesus Christ, I received the gift of eternal life. As a New Testament Jewish believer in Jesus Christ, I have promises of healing from Scripture. It is worth repeating from chapter 4, namely, that God heard my cries to him on the airplane flight home after Todd's severe traumatic brain injury, and diligently watched over me during times of deep distress. If we are believers and make a mistake like I did by not jogging against traffic, or failing to yield the right-of-way to other drivers, God will still be there for us!

As believers in Jesus Christ, you and I will make mistakes. If you have sinned and erred, be honest with yourself and the Lord. And remember that the apostle John's antidote for sin follows with a sobering truth. He writes, "If we confess our sins, He is faithful and just to forgive us *our* sins and to cleanse us from all unrighteousness. If we say that we have not sinned, we make Him a liar, and His word is not in us" (1 John 1:9–10). Even though I wasn't a believer at the age of eleven when I fell down the flight of stairs and sustained a concussion, God was watching over me and preparing my heart to receive his Son. It is important to note, God helps those who are unable to help themselves! I made several mistakes that should have killed me. However, God in his divine sovereignty foreknew this and helped me when I couldn't help myself. I have meditated on God's Word for preservation, guidance, and healing from physical affliction and therefore represent a living testimony of how God unconsciously leads a person to himself.

After accepting Jesus Christ as Savior, I realized that God intended for me to receive his blessings in order to boldly stand on his promises in the Bible. Aren't you glad God hasn't left us in the cold without a warm coat? Thank God we have the Holy Spirit, and the promises of God, particularly in the epistles, the letters to the church. There is healing in the Word of God for spiritual, emotional, and physical infirmities. It is worth repeating, I was saved by God's grace and healed by faith in the Word of God. *Yeshua HaMashiach* (Heb. Jesus the Messiah) not only healed me but changed my life, now and for all eternity. I am a Messianic Jew and definitely not ashamed of the gospel of Christ, for it represents the power of God to salvation, for me, a Jew, and also to the Greek (see Rom 1:16).

This Jewish sinner from Queens, New York, was saved, healed, and restored for service by the Lord. Therefore my perspective on human life transcends physical reality, while bordering on a divine periphery of existence.

LOOKING BEYOND THE SENSES[1]

I think it is fair to say that our human bodies, specifically the human brain's intricate yet efficient cerebral cortex, coupled with the limbic system and its superhighway of activity, transmits information though its synaptic pathways along the neurological periphery of life. Furthermore, the human senses enable people to believe that what they see, smell, taste, or hear encapsulates their dominant reality of life. My former seminary professor from Trinity Theological Seminary, Dr. Elbert E. Elliott, puts this in its proper perspective. He notes, "Life is always in the context of eternity."[2] This is a sobering reminder, particularly for unbelievers who put their faith and trust in themselves, a job, human wisdom, or other worldly ideas that contradict the Word of God. The unbeliever has unwittingly placed their faith and trust in a person, place, or thing.[3] The apostle Paul contends "that your faith should not be in the wisdom of men but in the power of God" (1 Cor 2:5). The bottom line is that man will fail us; the Lord does not! Human life is short compared to the life born-again believers will have with the risen Lord.[4] James's profound wisdom from chapter 4 of his epistle reminds us that human life is like a vapor that disappears because we live in a physical body, however, we do indeed possess a spirit and a soul (see Jas 4:14; 1 Thess 5:23).

It is noteworthy to recall the numerous apartment leases that I had signed over the years as a single believer in the Lord. The terms

1. Grossman, online participation post for Dr. Elliott's webinar "Evangelistic Preaching."

2. Elliott, "Evangelistic Preaching."

3. Grossman, online participation post for Dr. Elliott's webinar "Evangelistic Preaching."

4. Grossman, online participation post for Dr. Elliott's webinar "Evangelistic Preaching."

of the contract were always for one year, for I didn't own the apartment; it was temporarily used and rented until I was able to afford a permanent home. Nothing could prevent this lease from expiring because at the end of the year I was faced with signing another contract. My wife and I purchased a new home a number of years ago. We thought this resolved things, namely, that there wouldn't be coin-op laundry machines and, most importantly, there wouldn't be any leases to sign. Instead of being accountable to the apartment complex, my wife and I are now accountable to the bank for our home loan. If I escaped my apartment lease only to find permanent refuge in a beautiful home, do I have to worry about the lease expiring? People might say, "Gregg, you and your wife are in a new home; you don't have to worry about renewing year after year." The truth of the matter is that as long as we live in this physical life there will be afflictions (tests/trials). Nevertheless, we are reminded of the wonderful promise of the risen Lord, Jesus Christ. He declares, "These things I have spoken to you, that in Me you may have peace. In the world you will have tribulation; but be of good cheer, I have overcome the world" (John 16:33).[5]

The joyful reality for Christians is that God is so incredibly in love with us and the world that he gave people the opportunity to believe in Jesus Christ. And the blessings which follow from receiving Jesus Christ encapsulate a calm, peaceful soul. Paul writes, "Therefore, having been justified by faith, we have peace with God through our Lord Jesus Christ, through whom also we have access by faith into this grace in which we stand, and rejoice in hope of the glory of God" (Rom 5:1–2).

ETERNAL MUSINGS

Now that we have a taste of a heavenly viewpoint, let's return to the examples of the apartment and the home. If the apartment complex leaves several messages on my answering machine about my lease expiring, I am compelled to swiftly sign the lease and

5. Grossman, online participation post for Dr. Elliott's webinar "Evangelistic Preaching."

renew for another year. After all, I must do this because otherwise there wouldn't be any place for me to live. Yes, from a physical standpoint, I need a roof over my head. My former Sunday school teacher mentioned the short-lived time that we have on this earth. He exclaimed, "This is our temporary home." Remember, we are living and using these bodies for a short time. For instance, I recall meeting with a funeral home director for advertising several years ago. He said to me, in regards to people needing plans for funeral arrangements, "Gregg, it is not if, but when."[6] It is worth repeating the words of Dr. Elliott, for they encapsulate poignant depth and meaning, particularly for Christians, and for that matter the entire human race. He contends, "Life is always in the context of eternity."[7] Solomon, with all of his earthly wisdom, articulates a sobering yet profound truth from the Old Testament. He observes:

> He has made everything beautiful in its time. Also He has put eternity in their hearts, except that no one can find out the work that God does from beginning to end. (Eccl 3:11)[8]

We are reminded that death is not a matter of if, but when. Furthermore, your initial preparation for death remains in the "context of eternity."[9] Knowing this should compel us to proclaim to the people that God is not mad at them, but thankfully, he is madly in love with them! From the pulpit, we need to tell the unbeliever that after their lease is up, not only on their physical domicile, but on human life itself, that there is another *Landlord* (Jesus Christ) who will take us in and not throw us out (see John 6:37). If you are a homeowner, you are accountable to the bank for your mortgage, and if there is a default on the mortgage, you will incur hefty fines and fees from the lending institution. Through Jesus Christ, he has already paid the eternal fine through his atonement and death on

---

6. Grossman, online participation post for Dr. Elliott's webinar "Evangelistic Preaching."

7. Elliott, "Evangelistic Preaching."

8. Grossman, online participation post for Dr. Elliott's webinar "Evangelistic Preaching."

9. Elliott, "Evangelistic Preaching."

the cross. He paid it all, once and for all! It is our job as Christ's ambassadors (see 2 Cor 5:20) to beseech, urge, persuade, and proclaim to unbelievers in the world that they can receive a spiritual new birth that promises the gift of eternal life (see John 3:1–17).[10] May the Lord ignite our spirits by his Holy Spirit, enabling us to remember and boldly proclaim that "life is always in the context of eternity."[11]

LESSON IN ACTION

When Jesus Christ is your Lord and Savior, you have the assurance of eternity. Paul writes, "For we know that if our earthly house, *this* tent is destroyed, we have a building from God, a house not made with hands, eternal in the heavens" (2 Cor 5:1). What a wonderful promise from Paul! If you do not believe in Jesus Christ, would you consider looking beyond your human life toward eternity?

10. Grossman, online participation post for Dr. Elliott's webinar "Evangelistic Preaching."

11. Elliott, "Evangelistic Preaching."

12

Seeds of Forgiveness

And be kind to one another, tenderhearted, forgiving one
another, even as God in Christ forgave you.
—EPH 4:32

MATTER OF RECONCILIATION

My father brought my Bible and sermon tapes to me at the rehabilitation facility after my traumatic brain injury in 1992. In chapter
6 my father's friend and business colleague, the minister, arranged
for his church to pack up my apartment, for they loaded up the
furniture and my belongings were placed in storage. Dad divorced
his third wife, a woman who accepted, supported, and encouraged
me throughout their ten and a half years of marriage. My father and
I shared an apartment after this divorce and had the opportunity
to spend quality time together. Soon after moving into this apartment in a suburb of Fort Lauderdale, my father met a woman and
later remarried in Deerfield Beach, Florida. My father's new wife
and I had many differences, particularly regarding my faith in Jesus

Christ. The insidious process of separation and estrangement with Dad quickly accelerated as I grew in my Christian faith. After Dad's remarriage, his whole demeanor changed towards me. There was a radical metamorphosis with his behavior, for this deep bond of friendship, love, and support decayed, and much like a robust tree became devoid of vital, sustaining nutrients in my garden of life. This paternal relationship of thirty-one years, sadly, withered away.

After I moved to Texas, my father and I suspended all contact with each other, except for one telephone conversation in 2000. When Valerie and I became engaged in 2006, I reached out in confidence to my father's wife to share the great news. Shortly before the marriage ceremony, my father and I had a verbal disagreement over the telephone. Dad was intolerant, hurling profane, unsavory comments to me and to my then-fiancée, Valerie. Unfortunately, he did not attend my wedding in 2007 and we had not seen each other for many years. Although my father and I had a painful argument before the wedding, God was doing something special during the last seven years when we spoke on the telephone. Biblically, the number seven in the Hebrew Scriptures represents completion, for this was a lesson that I would draw upon in the months to come.

In March 2014, I received information from a family member that Dad's fourth wife had passed away. The years of silence between my father and me abruptly ended, for my niece provided his cell number, and with the love of Christ I dialed this number with sheer determination, hoping once again to reconnect with my father. We reconciled over the telephone and from this point forward his whole demeanor, attitude, and personality changed dramatically, for he was now the father that I knew well for many years. Furthermore, my father and I mutually forgave each other, for the latter were seeds of forgiveness that were sown to reconcile the differences from the estranged years. Dad stated, "Gregg, I learned to accept what you believe in and I am happy that you found meaning in life."

We talked almost every day on the telephone. My father mentioned to me that he contracted tongue cancer in December 2013 and shared that the radiation treatments had produced a remission of the disease. Moreover, this form of cancer required a tracheotomy and Dad contracted a respiratory infection which confined him to the hospital for several days. From his hospital bed, my dad found a one-bedroom apartment in another adult apartment community, and with the tenacity of a bull dog his friend helped him move into this apartment. My father's feisty yet determined personality resulted in discharging himself out of the hospital in order to move into this apartment. I greatly admired how my father was able to work through physical adversity in order to transition into making a life for himself.

A wedding photograph of Valerie and me under the *chuppah* (Heb., wedding canopy) at Baruch HaShem Messianic Synagogue, Dallas, Texas, May 19, 2007. The *tallit* (Heb., prayer shawl) from my *bar mitzvah* is hanging above.

THE REUNION

I reserved a plane ticket from Dallas, Texas, to South Florida in order to see my father in July 2014. As I left the baggage claim area, I walked outside because my dad informed me that he would be picking me up in front of the airport terminal. When his automobile approached the curb, the seat was reclined and it appeared like he was relaxing in a lounge chair. We spent several days together, for we reminisced about the good times and, conversely, we shared about the painful times of life. The companionship and deep bond that I had experienced with my father returned with a sweetness that deeply comforted my heart. Dad was a larger, portly man and the tongue cancer, his fourth wife's death, and the estrangement of me and my severely head-injured brother, Todd, I suspect resulted in excessive weight loss of about fifty pounds. Although somewhat emaciated in the upper torso, Dad had a raspy voice, experienced difficulty with walking, and required the use of a walker.

My time with Dad helped rebuild our mangled relationship. While in South Florida, I recall visiting with my friend, a fellow Jewish believer in Christ. Moreover, he took me to church and introduced me to the pastor after the service. I explained to him how God restored my relationship with my father. This kind pastor prayed with me after the church service and thanked the Lord for restoring the relationship with my father. A double blessing shortly followed, for my dear friend who had visited me in the hospital after I was critically injured in 1992 with a traumatic brain injury met me for lunch the following day. Mission accomplished! After several meaningful days visiting with my father, I experienced God's healing and restorative power of forgiveness. My father drove me to the airport and as we approached the airport terminal at Palm Beach International Airport, I reached over to my father, kissed him on the cheek, and said, "I love you." This was a lesson that I would reflect upon in the months to come.

My father and me at his apartment in South Florida, July 2014.

Upon returning to Dallas, Dad and I spoke every day on the telephone. Five months later, he traveled to Dallas to meet my wife, Valerie, and her folks. He received intensive physical therapy and was able to regain the mobility of his legs. Although he relied upon a cane, my father appeared well and full of vigor when my wife, Valerie, and I saw him in Dallas during the month of December 2014. He apologized to Valerie for his behavior seven years ago. The pinnacle of our time together occurred when my father met Valerie's parents, Fred and Joy Allen, at a restaurant in Arlington, Texas. Ironically, this was the same restaurant where my mother had met Fred and Joy Allen before Valerie and I married in 2007. During his short stay in Dallas, Dad and I spent one-on-one time talking about our lives. He told me that he was proud of me for my marriage to Valerie and greatly appreciated that I was part of a large family. Moreover, he shared memories about my brother Todd's severe traumatic brain injury in 1988. Dad's lucid memory about my traumatic brain injury in Florida reminded me about the Eternal Father who was manifested in Jesus Christ. At that moment, God's grace resonated throughout my being, while connecting heart to heart with my dad.

A NEW BEGINNING

The year 2015 looked like it was going to be a splendid year. I was in the second year of graduate study in the Master of Divinity program in pastoral ministry at Trinity Theological Seminary and my father was talking about planning another trip to Dallas, Texas, at the end of April. His voicemail in January stated that he was in the emergency room with an intense pain behind his eye. Dad stated that the hospital was running tests and that the physician gave him medication that relieved the symptoms and made him feel better. Moreover, my father informed me that he had lost another ten pounds. The physician urged Dad to drink a meal replacement drink in order to provide nourishment and increase his weight. Nonetheless, avoiding his physician's dietary instructions, Dad took matters in his own hands and bought ice cream to use with the meal replacement drink. On March 6, 2015, Dad's voicemail sounded like an excited kid who had hit a homerun out of the ballpark. With a joyful, elated tone, he stated, "Gregg, would you believe it? I gained ten pounds."

On March 18, 2015, I received a call in the late afternoon from Dad. He said that he had fallen and cracked his rib and was about to leave the hospital. My father said that he would call me back on my cell phone. Unfortunately I missed this call, for he left a message stating, "Gregg, call me when you have a minute." After I received this voicemail, I tried unsuccessfully to reach my father on his cell phone. I called Dad the following day, on Thursday, March 19, to check on him. After multiple attempts had failed to reach him by cell phone, I suspected something was wrong. Did my father fall and hit his head? Was he lying on the floor unconscious?

On Friday, March 20, I called the property management office at the adult community. They dispatched a senior security supervisor for a welfare check on my father. This security officer called me and I explained to him about my father's rib injury. Shortly thereafter, the senior security supervisor called me on my cell phone and explained that my father was coherent and lying in bed. The security officer was concerned about my father's breathing and recommended calling a paramedic. Dad's laborious breathing was from the cracked rib, or was it? I spoke with him on the telephone and with a frantic voice stated, "I have been worried sick about you. How are you feeling?" He replied, "I am very dizzy." I told Dad that he needed to have a paramedic look at him. His voice became forceful: "No, I don't want to; I am fine!" I concluded the telephone call by thanking this security officer for checking on my father and immediately placed a telephone call to Dad's friend, informing him about the fall. I asked this friend to check on my father and he told me that he would visit the apartment the following day, on Saturday around 6:00 p.m.

UNFORESEEN MOMENT

My cell phone rang several times after 5:00 p.m. Central Standard Time on Saturday, March 21, 2015. Dad's friend told me that he was at my father's apartment and stated, "Gregg, I have bad news for you. Your father is deceased." Deceased? How could that be? Panic and shock reverberated within my spirit, soul, and body, for I couldn't believe those words! As I began to process what had happened, I called my wife, Valerie, and she returned home immediately. My wife ordered the plane tickets on Sunday and we were scheduled to leave for West Palm Beach, Florida, on Wednesday, March 25, at 6:15 a.m. Two dear friends provided transportation to Dallas/Fort Worth International Airport. The memories of that early morning flight resembled the time on the airplane after my brother's automobile accident in chapter 4. Emotionally, my senses were overwhelmed as I tried to make sense of my father's death. This time, I knew the Lord and he moved me, much like that plane ride home from Vermont, to New York City after the severe traumatic brain injury of my brother, Todd. I was led to pick up the pen and pour out my heart to God. My journal captured this moment as the plane gracefully glided in the air from Dallas/Fort Worth International Airport towards Florida:

> It is 9:42 a.m. and we just lifted off from Dallas/Fort Worth International Airport. Deep within my heart, I recalled the feelings of devastation as I sat on that

airplane flight home from Vermont to be with my father after Todd's devastating car accident in 1988. My God looks upon me as I hurt deeply from this loss. I am writing this journal entry 23 years after I was saved. I declared his name, for I called upon the name of the Lord and he comforted me during the family tragedy. My deep communion with God on this flight to Florida resembled the aforementioned flight in 1988, for I found myself praying and resting in his loving care.

As I reflected upon the loss of my father, I discerned that he had gone home to be with the Eternal Father, the maker of heaven and earth (see Ps 146:6). I discerned Dad's spirit and soul within me, for he is a part of me. As this airplane journeyed to the land of South Florida, my spiritual birthplace, I was deeply comforted by the presence of God. During these painful moments of deep sadness and loss, I found great comfort digging into the Psalms and experiencing his Word minister to my despairing heart. My journal entry epitomized this communion as I opened my heart to God and prayed from the depths of my being:

> Heavenly father, I look to thee and my heart is comforted with thy loving kindness. Your mercies are new every morning and "great *is* thy faithfulness" [see Lam 3:22–23 KJV]. I loved my dad and I can now see how those seeds that I sowed in forgiveness brought You glory and ministered to dad 100-fold, for You were leading and guiding him home to You. I trust that I will see you again, dad. Jesus Christ has restored our relationship. Thank you for this day. This truly is the day that You have made. I rejoice in You! Dad, thank you for being you and for providing and supporting me over the years. God used you in a mighty way and I trust that you are rejoicing in heaven. Till I see you in the New Jerusalem. I love you, James J. Grossman! Lord, thank you for my father. I praise Your loving kindness that You have extended to me through your son, Jesus Christ. Amen.

Immediately after securing the rental car at the airport, we sped away towards I-95, the infamous freeway of the Floridian people. Our mission was to reach the funeral home in Palm Beach County in order to meet with the funeral home director. The grace of God overflowed as Valerie and I arranged for my father's cremation. Dad rented a one-bedroom apartment in an adult community. After we left the funeral home, Valerie and I headed to this apartment. As I unlocked the door and entered Dad's apartment, I visually observed the touch of a kind-hearted Christian woman who had cleaned his apartment every week for almost ten months. The living room looked immaculate. However, the kitchen counter reflected my father's difficulty with cleaning, for this dirty room spoke volumes about his physical and mental condition in the final hours of life. As I approached Dad's bedroom, I saw his king-size bed, and then a strange odor consumed my being, the smell of death.

FINAL CLOSURE

Every non-profit organization that I called throughout Palm Beach County stated that there was a one-week waiting period for a truck to haul away my father's furniture and belongings. Dismayed, I placed another call to a church that had a truck they used for picking up donated furniture. I shared with the dispatcher that my father had just passed away. After providing condolences for the loss, the dispatcher stated I should receive a telephone call the following morning from the delivery driver. The truck arrived the next day and hauled away most of my father's furniture. *Baruch HaShem!* (Heb., Bless the Name). Before the truck arrived at my father's apartment, Valerie and I spent most of the day packing up these belongings.

My friend, who provided the use of his home for me and my wife, called me and stated that he and his colleague were in the area and wanted to stop by the apartment to dispose of Dad's mattress. God knew the need even before we had this need. My friend and his business colleague carried my father's king-size mattress away with passionate urgency, and then with the strength of Sampson these two men hurled this king-size mattress over the railing of the second floor. Minutes later, they hauled away this death-smelling mattress to the recycling bin. My friend and colleague's kind, unexpected gesture played a huge role with emptying the apartment. We donated most of Dad's furniture and belongings to the church, while the Christian cleaning woman took the rest of my father's possessions. We cleaned out the apartment in about two days and God met every need during this time of loss. We serve a risen Savior who lives within and strengthens us in times of need (see 1 John 4:4; Phil 4:13).

As I exited Dad's apartment for the last time, I told my wife, Valerie, about needing a few minutes alone. I re-entered the apartment and proceeded to Dad's bedroom, then in a moment of contemplation, while gazing at the empty room, I walked over to the area of the room where the king-size bed once lay. I recall seeing the imprint on the tile floor of the legs from the king-size bed frame. I walked over to the left side of the room and imagined that my dad was lying on the bed. I bent over slightly and, with tears strolling down my face, I kissed his cheek and said, "I love you, Dad." This kiss on Dad's cheek reminded me of when I kissed him goodbye as I departed from his automobile at the airport terminal in South Florida, eight months ago. That latter kiss was a goodbye until I would see Dad five months later, while the former kiss, biblically, was a final, earthly goodbye until I myself step into eternity and joyfully embrace my earthly father, James J. Grossman, in the New Jerusalem (see Rev 21:9–21).

SEEDS OF THE GOSPEL

We arrived home in Dallas, Texas, on March 28 and it took time for the adrenaline and the shock of Dad's death to minimize. With that said, I gave myself the time and the space to grieve. I learned that grieving is not an event, but a painful process which requires going at my own pace during the healing process. My father's cremains arrived one week later from the funeral home in Florida. Easter was several days away and I recall the Lord ministering to me, for he provided spiritual insight about the death of my father, namely, that death produces reconciliation. For example, it is worth mentioning, my father's fourth wife passed away in March 2014. God used this death to reconcile me to my earthly father. Jesus, the divine Son of God, had to die and as a result reconciled us to his Father. This substitutionary atonement of Jesus Christ provided believers with "the ministry of reconciliation" (see 2 Cor 5:18–19). From this point forward, we can stand before the throne of God because he has removed our sins as they were cast from the east to the west (see Ps 103:12). This symbolic theme of reconciliation taught me that because Christ forgave me by dying on the cross at Calvary, I was able to forgive others, particularly my estranged father, who disowned me because of my faith in Christ. I began to understand that the forgiveness that was extended to my late father indeed represented seeds that were sown for the gospel. The forgiveness that Christ has given us is unmerited and incomprehensible to the human mind. Therefore these seeds of forgiveness towards my father made a positive impact in his life.

In the Gospel of John, a pivotal book that lies adjacent to the Synoptic Gospels, Jesus outlines this process of sowing, harvesting, and reaping (see John 4:35–38).[1] My friend, as you and I live out our faith, we too are planting fertile seeds in the lives of coworkers, family members, fellow brethren in the church, and, finally, the world at large. Hence these seeds invariably rest upon the soil of God. When I relocated to Dallas, Texas, there was a friend of my mother that said she respected my relocation to Texas. This woman, much like my father, viewed the world through the lens of Judaism. The late William Barclay, the eminent Scottish Bible scholar and author from the twentieth century, elucidates how my Jewish ancestors from the Hebrew Scriptures viewed this process of sowing.[2] Barclay's astute reasoning delves beneath the surface[3] of this parable, an earthly story containing a heavenly message, while emphasizing hermeneutical depth. He notes:

> To the Jew sowing time was a sad and a laborious time;
> it was harvesting time which was the time of joy. "They
> that sow in tears shall reap in joy. He that goeth forth

1. Barclay, *Gospel of John*, 160.
2. Barclay, *Gospel of John*, 161.
3. Barclay, *Gospel of John*, 161.

and weepeth bearing precious seed shall doubtless come again with rejoicing, bringing his sheaves with him" (*Psalm* 126:5, 6). But there is something else hidden below the surface here. The Jews had their dreams of the golden age, the age to come, the age of God, when the world would be God's world, when sin and sorrow would be done away with, and God would reign supreme. Amos paints his picture of it: "Behold the days come, saith the Lord, that the plowman shall overtake the reaper, and the treader of grapes him that soweth seed" (*Amos* 9:13). "Your threshing shall reach unto the vintage, and the vintage shall reach unto the sowing time" (*Leviticus* 26:5). It was the dream of that golden age that sowing and reaping, planting and harvesting, would follow hard upon the heels of each other. There would be such fertility that the old days of waiting would be at an end. So we see what Jesus is gently doing here. His words are nothing less than a claim that with Him the golden age has dawned; God's time is here; the time when the waiting is ended and the word is spoken and the seed is sown and the harvest waits.[4]

VALUED FARMER

As we engage in planting and sowing these seeds of the gospel, we become acutely aware about the perceptions of people, while our behaviors, actions, and attitudes find refuge within the subterranean depths of consciousness. Do you ever wonder how others perceive you? Years ago, my father opposed my faith in Jesus Christ vehemently, exclaiming, "You need to believe in your own religion" (Judaism). My father's tone reflected the pharisaic attitude of Christ's day. Was there hope for the seeds of the gospel to be sown in my father? I wholeheartedly believe that God fulfilled that hope through parental discord and adversity in life. After I was head-injured in 1992 and bedfast in the hospital, Dad brought me the Bible, for this living Word contains the footprint of Jesus Christ. If my father was discouraging

4. Barclay, *Gospel of John*, 161–62.

me from Christianity, then why would he willingly bring my Bible to the hospital? Was I planting seeds in my father's life that permeated his core of being? Unanimously, the answer is yes!

Judaism identifies me as part of God's chosen people. Hence legalism and rules without the atonement of Christ invariably produces frustration. It is worth repeating, this love and relationship with God through Jesus Christ produces freedom, for the Word became flesh, dwelt among the people, and sent his Holy Spirit to abide in you and me, therefore teaching, guiding, and instructing mankind with the "Spirit of truth" (see John 1:1, 14; 16:7–15). Moreover, when spiritual birth commences, we become valued farmers for the Lord. Heretofore, planting rewards us with rich dividends in our garden of life. Paul writes, "Now he who plants and he who waters are one, and each one will receive his own reward according to his own labor" (1 Cor 3:8). Finally, while we are planting the seeds of the gospel, many have endured opposition from obstinate family members such as parents, brothers, sisters, and other significant people in our lives. My friend, perhaps you too are like me and have been estranged from either your father or mother due to your faith in Christ. If you can relate to the aforementioned, then don't lose heart, but keep in mind that if your father or mother abandons you, God promises to take care of you (see Ps 27:10).

FAMILIAL RESTORATION

After I came to faith in Jesus Christ, my father told me that I had died and that he would say *Kaddish* (Mourner's Prayer). You may be grappling with domestic issues, parental discord, or even physical and emotional abuse. If your father or mother has passed away, then my grief speaks to your heart in a special way. For the reader whose family member is ill, and you have resentment or unresolved issues towards them, then this chapter, "The Seeds of Forgiveness," will challenge your thinking, while encouraging you to reconsider embracing your parent and loved ones. For those who are estranged from a parent or a loved one, particularly due to family or marital discord, please bow your head and let me pray for you:

Father in heaven, may your presence be with the reader who are estranged from their parent or loved ones. May your *Ruach HaKodesh* (Heb., Holy Spirit) comfort them, for your holy, written Word instructs us that this "yoke shall be destroyed because of the anointing" (see Isa 10:27, KJV). May your people take refuge in you and only you. "Your sandals *shall be* iron and bronze; As your days, *so shall* your strength *be* . . . The eternal God *is your* refuge, And underneath *are* the everlasting arms; He will thrust out the enemy from before you, And will say, 'Destroy!'" (Deut 33:25, 27). May they rest in God's tender, loving arms, for they are trusting in you, and only you, for reconciliation with their loved ones. In Jesus' name I pray, amen.

If your family member is terminally ill and you are at peace with them, then I want you to know that I sincerely empathize with you. My wife lost her older brother, Gary, aged fifty-four, to lung cancer in June 2014. Although he was a Christian, the loss of a sibling is painfully hard to process, for this too, much like a parent, involves a deep cohesive bond emanating to the earliest time in our lives. I have the blessed assurance that I will see my father again in heaven. He will be eating his favorite delicacy, hard salami, without any dietary concerns. My friend, I don't know the relationship that you have with your mother or father. However, I want to tell you that God used them in a mighty way to bring you into this world. I was close with my dad while growing up in New York. We had a special bond and he once remarked, "You are so much like me." My father, deep down within his being, loved me, irrespective of the divorce with Mom, the multiple failed marriages, and his resistance to my faith in Jesus Christ. Although it feels like I lost my best friend, the deep pain, grief, and bereavement humbled me and drew me closer to my Lord (see Jas 4:8). Finally, it is evident that the sovereign hand of God, the sustainer and author of life, called Dad home. My father is free from physical and emotional pain and is experiencing peace with his dad, the Eternal Father.

LESSON IN ACTION

With life there is hope, for we must, before leaving this earth, reconcile ourselves to God through Jesus Christ. If things aren't right with your mother, father, siblings, or other family members, I urge you to reconcile with them. It is worth repeating these vital words from chapter 10, for when we forgive loved ones, friends, or other people, it is then and only then that we will receive from God (see Matt 6:14). When you submit your life to God through Jesus Christ, this empowers you to reconcile with family members. Are there family or friends with whom you need to make amends? Why not commit this to prayer right now.

In Loving Memory
James J. Grossman
8/28/31—3/21/2015

13

In Retrospect

But we all, with unveiled face, beholding as in a mirror the
glory of the Lord, are being transformed into the same image
from glory to glory, just as by the Spirit of the Lord.

—2 COR 3:18

GOD'S TIMING

After moving to Dallas, Texas, in 1998 to attend Dallas Theological Seminary, I understood why the seminary's academic program wasn't the right fit or timing in life. Furthermore, I didn't have a church home at that time, and as a believer in Jesus Christ I earnestly desired God's will for my life. And when the door of opportunity closed to pursue graduate studies at Dallas Theological Seminary, I learned from the experience that "when God says 'no,'" this means redirection.[1] My friend, have you ever endeavored to accomplish goals in your life only to find that your plans never materialized? Does getting back on the horse after falling or stumbling in life

1. Swindoll, Charles R. "When God Says 'No,'" 7.

mean that we eventually succeed? If it is the Lord's will, then it shall be (see Jas 4:15). My faith in God through Jesus Christ, coupled with Norwich University's motto, "I will try," permanently engraved itself within the recesses of my heart. I believe that the biggest obstacles in human life are not diseases, accidents, indifference, or even bitterness of the human heart. The most insurmountable obstacle facing the twenty-first-century citizen lies in the ability to trust the Creator, the transcendent, omnipotent, and sovereign God who became manifest in Jesus Christ. My heart pleads, "Lord, help that impatient soul realize that emotions are indeed a poor barometer for making decisions." And this leads me to ask: How do you deal with patience? Many of us struggle in this area, while others seem to possess an impenetrable fortitude and demeanor that keeps them going despite the circumstances. James, the half-brother of Christ, pastored a church in Jerusalem and provides a timeless lesson exemplifying godly, mature wisdom for the sanctified believer in Jesus Christ, while challenging unbelievers to consider the value of adversity. James writes,

> My brethren, count it all joy when you fall into various trials, knowing that the testing of your faith produces patience. But let patience have *its* perfect work, that you may be perfect and complete, lacking nothing. If any of you lacks wisdom, let him ask of God, who gives to all liberally and without reproach, and it will be given to him. (Jas 1:2–5)

I can imagine that your diastolic and systolic blood pressure numbers have climbed erratically after hearing the word "perfect" (v. 4). The two instances of the word "perfect" (Gr., *teleios*) that are used by James convey the idea of being morally complete. When the rubber band of your faith is stretched beyond the maximum threshold, patience reaches the finish line and it is during those precious, trying moments that we remember God's promise to Job, "But He knows the way that I take; *When* He has tested me, I shall come forth as gold . . ." (Job 23:10). God is chiseling away at the human heart and preparing us to live and walk on this path called life. It is important to remember the unexpected peaks, valleys, turbulence, and, yes, the accomplishments, for the former challenges our patience, while the latter makes the process sweeter to the human soul. I recall the iconic chant from summer camp as the young, enthusiastic campers emphatically chanted aloud from their viscera, "What do we want?" With powerful emotion, the campers yelled their intrinsic needs, while momentarily, with the ephemeral beat of time, they continued their shouting by asking, "When do we want it?" Finally, their conditioned response exclaimed, "We want it now!" Simply put, we live in a microwave culture that teaches people that if they immediately want a beverage or a meal then they place the desired item in a mechanical contrivance called a microwave, set the timer for the desired time, and then minutes later with expected anticipation, salivate like a Pavlovian dog with parched mouth and hungry stomach, while quickly grabbing this beverage or meal which satisfies their intrinsic, biological need for nourishment. Furthermore, this microwave culture of society expects instant gratification for its needs. And we behave like those campers who vehemently demand, "We want it now!"

Maybe you have put your hand to the plow, much like the diligent farmer who faithfully attended the fields every morning for years. Convinced that the timing was right and the fruit was ripe for harvest, like the farmer, you confidentially sowed seeds in your education, business, health, finances, or relationships. Figuratively speaking, as you bit into that seemingly ripe piece of fruit, you shattered every tooth in your mouth. Not only would this require an exorbitant expense to the cosmetic dentist, the failed attempt would leave anyone discouraged, frustrated, angry, disillusioned, and unsure about trying again. Hence, navigating through life's vicissitudes to "live beyond perseverance" requires the understanding that the vicarious atonement of the Suffering Servant became the fulfillment to the gospel of Christ, the power of salvation to transform lives on earth (see especially Isa 52:13–53:12; Rom 6:5–6; Eph 4:17–24).

For those who believe in the death, burial, and resurrection of Jesus Christ, you possess his Word, his Holy Spirit, and the epistolary guidelines that govern your actions, attitudes, and behaviors in life. The aforementioned, indeed, stand diametrically in relation to those wrestling with or opposing the deity of Christ. With that said,

Paul writes, "For the message of the cross is foolishness to those who are perishing, but to us who are being saved it is the power of God" (1 Cor 1:18). If you are of the Jewish faith or from another religious belief system, please consider the following statement with an open heart and an open mind. The divine seed, specifically the messianic prophetic utterance from the Jewish prophet Isaiah (see Isa 9:6–7), not only became consummated through Jesus Christ in the Synoptic Gospel narratives, but was inspired by the Holy Spirit in the Pauline corpus of the New Testament. Finally, it is imperative to provide a biblical framework to this word "perseverance," and that is what I intend to do in the next section.

DYNAMICS OF PERSEVERANCE

The person who endeavors to "live beyond perseverance," notably believers in Jesus Christ, must not only consider the psychological and philosophical ingredients, but also, it becomes imperative to maintain a biblical doctrine of the human condition. First, man is a sinner who is in need of a Savior, Jesus Christ. As I mentioned in chapter 6, people cannot save themselves, for the latter has been accomplished through the death, burial, and resurrection of Jesus Christ. His sacrificial death on the cross represented salvation for the sins of mankind (see Gen 3:1–24; Rom 3:23; 10:8–9; Eph 2:8–9; John 3:16–17).[2] There will be times when you want to quit and may say to yourself, "I can't do this anymore," namely, due to being physically, emotionally, or spiritually challenged. Take a lesson from the disciple Peter, for his words breathe life and hope into a weary soul. He writes, "Therefore humble yourselves under the mighty hand of God, that He may exalt you in due time, casting all your care upon Him, for He cares for you" (1 Pet 5:6–7).

As I indicated earlier in the chapter, the most insurmountable obstacle facing the twenty-first-century citizen is the ability to trust the Creator. Therefore the second rudimentary principle for "living beyond perseverance" will require you to relinquish your burdens by submitting to God. If you are going to trust God, then you must

2. See "Christian Life Coaching" at beyondperseverance.com.

relinquish every thought to the obedience of Christ (see 2 Cor 10:5). Adele Ahlberg Calhoun, author of the *Spiritual Disciplines Handbook: Practices That Transform Us*, explains the meaning and spiritual value of this word "submission." She writes, "Submission that leads to growth means aligning my will and freedom with God's will and freedom. God's will for us includes freely submitting to each other out of love and reverence for Christ."[3] As you allow this word "submission" to penetrate your soul, I want to ask you a question, and please be honest with yourself and God: Are you submitted to Jesus Christ?

I think it is fair to say that adopting an attitude of humility while going the extra mile for others yields rich dividends in the kingdom of God. Third, "living beyond perseverance" will require serving God and serving others in life. This means that if you want to serve the Lord, then you will have to serve your employer. That's right, I mean submitting to the authority of your boss at your place of employment. Paul writes, "Let as many bondservants [*employees*] as are under the yoke count their own masters [*bosses*] worthy of all honor, so that the name of God and *His* doctrine may not be blasphemed" (1 Tim 6:1; insertions and emphasis mine). Furthermore, I want to encourage you to serve God, the community, and the totality of human life, namely, mankind. Working as a chaplain, minister, and a Christian life coach has enabled me to pour my life into others, for the latter redefined my life as a Jewish believer in Christ, while affirming the value of selfless service toward people. Mark's Gospel provides a foundational truth about service. Christ states, "For even the Son of Man did not come to be served, but to serve, and to give His life a ransom for many" (Mark 10:45). It is important to understand the biblical framework behind the dynamics of perseverance because it provides insight for navigating the peripheral straits of life. After you have prayed, maybe cried, or for that matter vented, you are now at a critical juncture in the process of perseverance, namely, you believe in your mind and heart that you have indeed done your best in the situation.

3. Calhoun, *Spiritual Disciplines Handbook*, 118.

RELEASE THE OUTCOME

Finally, the last step with "living beyond perseverance" means that it is time to let go of the thoughts or feelings that were associated with the effort. Yes, I mean step away, leave it with God and move onward. This is a critical part of the process because you must keep moving, even in the trenches of despair. May the Holy Spirit produce a laser-sharp focus, gazing upon your calling to be the person God has called you to be in life. Paul writes, "Not that I have already attained, or am already perfected; but I press on, that I may lay hold of that for which Christ Jesus has also laid hold of me" (Phil 3:12). When it is all said and done, namely, your confession of sin and trust in Christ for salvation by faith, this reveals Christlikeness, notably a willingness to submit to him by serving others. And because you trust Christ with the outcome, you can rest confidentially, knowing that you have fulfilled his will for your life. As you "live beyond perseverance," and remain true to God, true to his Word, and true to his people, when you take your last breath of life and enter eternity, may Christ's words of obedience welcome you home: "'Well *done*, good and faithful servant; you have been faithful over a few things, I will make you ruler over many things. Enter into the joy of your lord'" (Matt 25:23).

I travelled over fifteen hundred land miles to find that God redirected my path in life. I have learned that redirection and delay for the things we genuinely desire in life yield fruit that produces blessings for a lifetime. Since the writing of this final chapter, God used my pastor and friend, Dr. Charles L. Wilson, in a mighty way. For example, during the summer of 2013, he asked me if I wanted to participate in a pastoral leadership class that was held at a church several miles from my house. He served on the board of regents at Trinity College of the Bible and Theological Seminary and invited me to an all-day lecture at a local church. In retrospect, shortly after the mild traumatic head injury in 2011, I prayed with Dr. Wilson in his office about a door to open for higher education. I thought that graduate school, or for that matter any form of schooling, was finished in my life. However, the Lord had other plans.

After the pastoral leadership seminar, I enrolled in the accelerated Master of Divinity program at Trinity Theological Seminary. Majoring in pastoral ministry, I became a long-distance student learner, taking all-day live webinars that enabled me to complete courses in five weeks. Moreover, I took live webinars that met in the evening and lasted for four weeks. Finally, I had a church home and the support and prayers from people, and made a covenant with the Lord to finish this program. With that said, I learned to release the outcome by trusting God to persevere.

STORMS, BUT SUNSHINE

I think it is fair to say that answered prayer never promised life without storms. For example, my wife, Valerie, and I endured painful loss and tragedy during graduate school. She pursued an MBA, while I pursued this graduate degree with fervor. Valerie's brother, Gary, was diagnosed with lung cancer and my precious wife, shortly after Gary's terminal diagnosis, developed blood clots in her leg and lung. Moreover, my wife lost her brother to cancer and nine months later my father passed away suddenly. The love and prayers from our church family became the glue that truly held us together during these difficult days. If it weren't for the love of Christ, his Word, or the loving church family members, I would have, much like a flower without sunshine or water, wilted and faded away into oblivion. The Lord envelops our lives, using people to comfort us during times of tragedy. It is worth repeating, Psalm 34:19 states, "Many *are* the afflictions of the righteous, But the LORD delivers him out of *them all*" (emphasis added). God never promised deliverance from some trials or from even a few. My God promised deliverance from them all! The Lord healed my wife, Valerie, and also healed and restored me for service. I started the final lap for the Master of Divinity degree, a pastoral ministry practicum at a church outside of the Dallas–Fort Worth metroplex, and I could see the finish line for the graduate degree. However, there was another prerequisite to my seminary training that wasn't listed in the seminary's online course curriculum.

As I continued working in outside sales, I decided to return home to make follow-up calls one afternoon in November 2015. As I drove the Honda Accord home, my car and an eighteen-wheeler collided on the freeway. Within the blink of an eye, I found myself in another near-death experience. I was terrified and waited on the shoulder of the freeway for the police. Numb and shaken, I slid out of the automobile and noticed that the eighteen-wheeler had decimated the side paneling of the driver's door. Nevertheless, I drove the car to my auto body shop, parked the car, and then my wife, Valerie, transported me to the rental car office. While sitting in the waiting area, I recall the intense fear reverberating through my soul. From my heart, I cried out to God, "Was this accident my fault? God, how could this happen?" Below the threshold of awareness, I discerned the psalmist's feverish question, "God, why?" It is worth repeating this pivotal verse of Scripture from earlier in the book, for the stillness of the moment, without a doubt, reflected King David's realization that during moments of despair, stillness before God will indeed prevail (see Ps 46:10). The Holy Spirit breathed hope into me. For his still small voice whispered to my soul, "You are the healed of the LORD. My will shall be fulfilled for your life" (see Exod 15:26; Isa 46:10).

After hearing from the Lord in the rental car waiting area, I recall searching Scripture like a Berean (see Acts 17:11) and found confirmation in the Old Testament. I knew with certainty that God's will was being fulfilled in my life. And I knew because the Lord spoke the Word to my soul. This profound moment fueled my mind and body with an indefatigable zeal to complete this graduate degree.

INTERPRETING EXPERIENTIAL PHENOMENA

The interrelationship between the body and life experiences appear discernible along the landscape of human existence.[4] The late Christian philosopher Dallas Willard explains,

---

4. Willard, *Renovation of the Heart*, 161.

THEREFORE MY BODY is the original and primary place of *my dominion* and my responsibility. It is only through it that I have a *world* in which to live. That is why it, and not other physical objects in my world, is part of who I am and is essential to my identity. My life experiences come to me through or in conjunction with my body.[5]

I recall the early years of life growing up in the temperate climate of the Northeast. New York City reminded me that the autumn months meant the start of school, the High Holy Days of *Rosh Hashanah* and *Yom Kippur*, followed by the onset of winter precipitation, namely, snow and the formation of ice on the roads. Spring meant relinquishing the winter coat and opting for lighter clothes, while the summertime produced scorching temperatures outside, where the humidity was so thick you could cut it with a knife. The variegated fluctuations of the temperature invariably reflect a deeper meaning along the panorama of life. Solomon characterizes this profundity, notably, the breadth and depth of seasonal life activity (see Eccl 3:1–8). Hence the diametric yet environmental milieu on earth represents a symbolic manifestation of cyclic intervals throughout the life span. Charles R. Swindoll provides a dynamic yet lucid picture of the extrinsic variables to life, while chronicling the experiential components of human existence. He writes:

> Our journey begins in the winter, a season of quiet *reverence*. This is followed by spring, a season of refreshing and encouraging *renewal*. Then comes summer, a season of enjoyable and much-needed *rest*. Finally, we'll stroll through autumn, a season of nostalgic *reflection*. Our hope is to grow stronger and taller as our roots dig deeper in the soft soil along the banks of the river of life. And let's not fear the winds of adversity![6]

And remember, the momentary lapse of affliction which tests your patience invariably precedes life breakthrough, for God is at work behind the scenes in your life, and when the intermission of

5. Willard, *Renovation of the Heart*, 161.

6. See Swindoll, *Growing Strong in the Seasons of Life*, "Introduction," 13.

adversity runs its course, God opens the curtain, revealing a portrait of things to come. This was the case with me towards the end of graduate school at Trinity Theological Seminary. For the latter typified the quintessential mode of being, namely, the catalyst for theological growth in the days ahead.

JEWISH REAWAKENING

During the writing of this book, I recalled a messianic rabbi's words, challenging yet intriguing. He stated, "Gregg, you have a Jewish identity." Those six words became pivotal seeds that germinated within the inner depths of my soul. My heart exclaimed, "Oh *Avraham, Yitzhak,* and *Ya'akov* [Heb., Abraham, Isaac, Jacob], my beloved patriarchs of the faith, the words from the *Torah,* coupled with Moses, Isaiah, Jeremiah, Ezekiel, Daniel, and the twelve Minor Prophets, have reawakened my Jewishness." First, it was an honor and a blessing to have studied at Trinity Theological Seminary, an esteemed theological institution. Second, my Jewish reawakening was triggered by the reading, research, and writing of my doctoral dissertation. This rigorous yet deeply meaningful research endeavor strengthened my Jewish roots, stimulated my Jewish identity, and facilitated a love for all Jewish people and *Eretz Yisrael* (Heb., Land of Israel). Third, it is even a greater blessing for a traditional Jew to come to faith in Jesus Christ. I am proud to be a Messianic Jew and when you receive Jesus Christ as Lord and Savior, you never lose your Jewish identity! Messianic Jewish scholar Dr. David Rudolph explains:

> The realization that Yeshua is the Messiah of Israel, the one foretold by the prophets of Israel, is often followed by a second life-transforming realization: that the God of Israel calls Jews who follow the Jewish Messiah to remain Jews and become better Jews in keeping with his eternal purposes.[7]

7. See David Rudolph, "Introduction," 11, in Rudolph and Willitts, eds., *Introduction to Messianic Judaism.*

I wholeheartedly concur with Dr. Rudolph's observation in the preceding paragraph. Therefore it is my humble opinion that believing in Jesus Christ never means the relinquishing of Jewishness! Hence my born-again experience in 1992 represented an extension of my Jewishness, while the life-long process of sanctification and discipleship from the teachings of *Yeshua* (Heb., Jesus) continue till the last breathe of life. Furthermore, I have discerned that being a Jewish believer in Jesus Christ encapsulates a deeply held conviction transcending conscious awareness. God, the almighty Creator in *Yeshua* produced an indelible imprint within my Jewish soul. For the latter transcends the epistemological planes of inquiry, while the former borders the divine will of the risen, sovereign Lord. Finally, it is worth repeating the messianic rabbi's statement from earlier in this section, because "Jewish identity" typifies the embodiment of a sacred heritage, for the Jewish people epitomize resilience along the historiographical landscape of life, while underscoring their perpetual survival for existence. If you are Jewish, then my words speak to you in a meaningful way. You recognize the indefatigable yet irrefutable quest of God's chosen people to survive, especially in the midst of antisemitism. May the psalmist's invitation call you to worship the One God of Abraham, Isaac, and Jacob manifested through Jesus Christ:

> Oh come, let us worship and bow down;
> Let us kneel before the LORD our Maker.
> For He *is* our God,
> And we *are* the people of His pasture,
> And the sheep of His hand. (Ps 95:6–7)

SPIRITUAL PERSEVERANCE

I remember my late father's presence at graduation from Norwich University on May 18, 1991. Now, twenty-five years later, I would be walking in commencement without Dad. On August 6, 2016, I recall walking to the stage at the Thomas R. Rodgers Center in Newburgh, Indiana. Moments before my name was called to receive the graduate diploma, I looked at the meaningful symbols from the gold graduation ring from Norwich University, a college in the Green Mountain State. The engraving on this ring, "I WILL TRY," warmed my heart with joy as I thanked the Lord and walked across the stage to receive the Master of Divinity degree in pastoral ministry. My graduate professor who was on the podium silently muttered, "Congratulations, Gregg." My friend, this life is short, and trivial events in life won't matter a second in eternity. God took this precocious Reform Jewish boy from Queens, New York, and protected his life from the anguish of parental divorce, severe brain injury of a family member, and finally my own traumatic brain injuries. Moreover, God was drawing me to himself and enabled me to survive painful life tragedies, sustaining and healing me for service. The vital component personifying these times of perseverance invariably lies in Jesus Christ. Paul writes:

> Blessed *be* the God and Father of our Lord Jesus Christ, who has blessed us with every spiritual blessing in the heavenly *places* in Christ, just as He chose us in Him before the foundation of the world, that we should be holy and without blame before Him in love, having predestined us to adoption as sons by Jesus Christ to Himself, according to the good pleasure of His will, to the praise of the glory of His grace, by which He made us accepted in the Beloved. (Eph 1:3–6)

I am accepting the Master of Divinity degree in pastoral ministry from
Dr. Braxton Hunter, president of Trinity College of the Bible and
Theological Seminary, August 6, 2016.

My wife, Valerie, took this photo at the commencement ceremony
on August 6, 2016.

THREE INSIGHTS TO CONSIDER

I learned valuable wisdom in *Yeshua HaMashiach* (Heb., Jesus the Messiah) and believe that these life lessons will challenge your thinking, while stimulating your faith. You might be saying to yourself, "How is that going to transpire?" It would behoove you to consider the three spiritual horizons of mankind. First, people desire life purpose and therefore possess a yearning along the periphery of the soul to have communion with God, the Creator. Second, human beings possess an unquenchable hunger for deep meaning in their lives. Finally, it is worth reiterating, every man and woman inhabiting the earth will have to stand before the holy God to give an account of their life (see Heb 9:27). My friend, are you prepared to stand before God to give this account? Do you have a purpose for your life? Are you doing what God has called you to do and being what God has called you to be? If you answered yes to these questions, then I rejoice, knowing that you are truly a child of God. However, if you answered no, then please reread chapter 9, "Saved, Not by Accident." May this chapter find peace for your soul.

CONNECTING WITH WOUNDED SOULS

As mentioned in the introduction, the purpose for writing this book has been to not only share my strength, inspiration, and hope to the brain-injured and their families, but to present the gospel of Jesus Christ to the physically, emotionally, and spiritually wounded of society. I might add that being a survivor of grief, which was attributed to personal and family traumatic brain injury, has enabled me as a licensed Southern Baptist minister, bivocational workplace chaplain, and a Christian life coach to understand the depth of human suffering. Hence I am gifted to connect with a suffering soul through the medium of writing. Since this book will pass through many hands throughout the world, I approach the painful wounds of the human condition with sensitivity, but am aware that this depraved, elemental feature contains a rich reservoir of wisdom, notably, the healed scars from my times of perseverance on the battlefields of life. Furthermore, connecting with the reader on a deeper level through transparent sharing provides a conduit of hope, inspiration, and encouragement, while challenging their thinking and prompting them toward action. The latter synthesizes the intricacies of human experience, while the former reaches the deepest needs of people, namely, their unspoken pain and tragedies, which lie suppressed below the threshold of awareness. My heartfelt prayer is that you become blessed as you prevail through insurmountable obstacles in life. As life draws to a close, may the Holy Spirit's inspired Word spoken through the apostle Paul to his young disciple Timothy rejuvenate your soul. He writes:

> I have fought the good fight, I have finished the race, I have kept the faith. Finally, there is laid up for me the crown of righteousness, which the Lord, the righteous Judge, will give to me on that Day, and not to me only but also to all who have loved His appearing. (2 Tim 4:7–8)

CONCLUDING REMARKS

When we endure the pain of physical, emotional, spiritual, financial, and interpersonal afflictions, human limitations impede our ability to see God's sovereign plan. Simply put, we cannot see our situation the way God sees it when we are going through life adversity. Furthermore, we are unable to see the outcome of everything we are doing. Nevertheless, I have encouraging news for you. God does! For the Lord Jesus Christ sees the beginning and the end (see Rev 22:13). And at some point you can look back at that painfully challenging event and mutter silently, "Ah yes, Lord, I can see why that happened to me." And let me add, if there has been a horrific event in your life, you may never be able to comprehend why it happened. Nevertheless, keep in mind that it has made you into the person that you are today. Second, life adversity isn't happening to you, but for you in order to prepare you for the days ahead. Third, I want to encourage you that God is aware of your life and that he desires you to relinquish your burdens and sins to his care. If you are enduring a life hardship, let me encourage you to consider that the completion of your faith lies in Jesus Christ. The writer of Hebrews explains:

> Therefore we also, since we are surrounded by so great a cloud of witnesses, let us lay aside every weight, and the sin which so easily ensnares *us*, and let us run with endurance the race that is set before us, looking unto Jesus, the author and finisher of *our* faith, who for the joy that was set before Him endured the cross, despising the shame, and has sat down at the right hand of the throne of God. (Heb 12:1–2)

Fourth, this journey called life is paved with unexpected challenges and at times insurmountable obstacles, namely, disease, fear, worry, despair, solitude, and grief, to name a few. Perhaps you are at a place in your life that is consumed by sin. You may have shed an infinite amount of tears, and frankly you may feel sick and tired of being sick and tired. The latter typifies the insidious process of sin, while the former represents a sorrowful heart. If you are at that point in your life, take note of David's transparent cry to God. He writes:

> Have mercy upon me, O God,
> According to Your lovingkindness;
> According to the multitude of Your tender mercies,
> Blot out my transgressions.
> Wash me thoroughly from my iniquity,
> And cleanse me from my sin.
>
> For I acknowledge my transgressions,
> And my sin *is* always before me.
> Against You, You only, have I sinned,
> And done *this* evil in Your sight—
> That You may be found just when You speak,
> *And* blameless when You judge. (Ps 51:1–4)

In the psalm of David from the preceding paragraph you hear a transparent heart revealing sin to God. Therefore, this serves as a reminder for us to consider the condition of our heart when approaching and confessing sins to God. Finally, I found great comfort in the late Billy Graham's book *Hope for the Troubled Heart*, for it ministered to me after Todd's severe traumatic brain injury, and it is my sincere hope that it does the same for you. Graham writes:

> When we are weak and powerless, God is there to give us strength. When we lack wisdom, He will supply it. Healing is not instantaneous; it is a process. When we admit that we cannot heal ourselves, and we fall to our knees and ask God to take over, we will be on the road to spiritual health. Why wait?[8]

Are you ready to take the first step? You can do it! God does the rest . . .

LESSON IN ACTION

When you "live beyond perseverance," God will help you to relinquish life outcomes because he is in more control of your life than you could ever imagine, for he is working below your threshold of conscious awareness (see Phil 1:6). May the following words from the book of Proverbs challenge your thinking, stir your soul, and prompt you to action. Solomon writes:

> Trust in the Lord with all your heart,
> And lean not on your own understanding;
> In all your ways acknowledge Him,
> And He shall direct your paths. (Prov 3:5–6)

8. Graham, *Hope for the Troubled Heart*, 126.

14

Postscript

The Silent Invader

Grief is unavoidable, a painful reality of life.

—GREGG L. GROSSMAN, PHD,

PRESIDENT OF BEYOND PERSEVERANCE LLC[1]

UNCOMMON TIMES

As I worked diligently to finalize this manuscript, a global pandemic has ravaged the face of the earth and disguised itself like the odorless, colorless gas of carbon monoxide, undetectable to the physical senses. COVID-19 personified the new norm within the vernacular of global society. Moreover, this unprecedented public health crisis has impaired the economy, altered life routine, and stretched the hospital system to maximum overload. Life as we have known it to be remains at a surreal, immoveable standstill, while the fear of contracting this highly contagious virus permeates the soul of mankind. This precious gift called life stands juxtaposed with the christological foreshadowing of pestilences (see Matt 24:7b). The

1. See beyondperseverance.com

coronavirus echoes Christ's prophetic utterance in the Synoptic Gospels, reminding humanity that we are living in the last days before his glorious return.

Life routine for the global citizen has been drastically altered by the coronavirus. Consequentially, many people, including myself, have lost their jobs, are burdened with paying bills, and struggle to provide for their families. Life before this insidious virus's attack typified an innocuous existence amidst the vicissitudes of life, while its undetectable array of deleterious pathogens coalesced, initiating a toxic wildfire throughout the earth. Consequentially, this engulfed into a raging, silent invader, propelling this highly communicable virus to spread expeditiously throughout the global domain. Frankly, there isn't one person who hasn't been impacted by the coronavirus. Many who are reading either have contracted the coronavirus, know of someone with it, or sadly, have lost a loved one to this respiratory plague. If you have lost a loved one or someone close, you certainly are not alone.

MANAGEABLE AILMENT

It was a typical gastrointestinal, episodic moment for my mother, Lee Grossman. She suffered with spastic colitis for forty-five years, while the onset of irritable bowel syndrome and diverticulitis appeared later in life. My mother seemed to be a veteran of chronic, lifelong gastrointestinal challenges, always recovering with the resiliency of a bulldog. The first few months of 2020 were difficult for Mom. She was bleeding internally in the gastrointestinal tract and as a result her hemoglobin dropped considerably, requiring monitoring by the physician. Her gastroenterologist ordered an emergency endoscopy to determine if the source of the bleeding was caused by an arteriovenous malformation. The physician who performed this procedure revealed that there wasn't bleeding in the upper gastrointestinal tract. However, after testing mom's hemoglobin, the physician discovered that it dropped to a dangerously low level. Furthermore, the doctor sent her to the emergency room immediately for a blood transfusion. There was the possibility that the gastrointestinal bleed was caused by the diverticulitis. With that said, my mother received a blood transfusion, was admitted into the hospital, and was scheduled for the next available colonoscopy. During this procedure, it revealed an enormity of stool, and this prevented the doctor's scope from identifying the potential bleed in the colon. This procedure was so invasive for my mother that the gastroenterologist would subject her to it only in an emergency.

Upon returning home the following day, I instructed my mother to call the grocery store for food because the coronavirus was rampant throughout New York City and the surrounding boroughs. When we spoke on the telephone, Mom informed me that she went out for basic essentials at the grocery store and would call the grocery store to order food. As the days progressed, Mom informed me that she was having chronic black stools, an indication of internal bleeding. After visiting the gastroenterologist's office several blocks from home, her blood was retested, and it revealed that her hemoglobin was once again low, requiring another blood transfusion. My mother was terrified about going to the emergency room and contracting the coronavirus. Feelings of helplessness consumed my being, and my only choice in this matter was to research clinics that provided blood transfusions. However, at the time of this public health crisis they closed their doors of operation. Miraculously, the bleeding ceased, however, on Friday, March 27, Mom's neighbor friend visited her apartment and remarked, "Lee, you don't look good. You need to go to the hospital." The neighbor called 911 and Mom was picked up by an ambulance and rushed to a local hospital. I spoke with my mother on the telephone and was informed that she was receiving another blood transfusion in the emergency room. After the blood transfusion she was admitted into the hospital. I let my mother rest and planned to follow up with her the following day.

I called my mother on Saturday, March 28, after lunch and she told me that she was in isolation with a fever over 102 degrees. She stated, "I feel like Typhoid Mary. You should see what's going on here." We spoke on the telephone and then I let her get some rest. I called the hospital in the early evening to talk with the nurse. She told me that Mom's fever was normal and that her vital signs were good. I asked the nurse, "Why did she have a fever?" She informed me that this could have been due to the anemia. I felt relieved and told the nurse that I would be calling tomorrow to talk with my mom.

MATTER OF MISCOMMUNICATION

It was Sunday, March 29, and I had waited till after lunch to call the hospital. When I called the main desk, I asked to be transferred to my mother's room. After I gave her name and birthdate, the operator told me that there wasn't any record of her in the database. I was transferred to the hospital unit where Mom had been placed upon admittance into the hospital. Once again, I mentioned the room number to the administrative assistant and she put me on hold. At this time, I had the telephone call on speaker phone, and when the assistant returned to the phone she informed me that the attending physician needed to talk with me. She commented, "Didn't the hospital call you?" I looked at my wife, Valerie, and she said, "This doesn't sound good."

When the doctor got to the phone, she began the conversation by telling me that my mother's hemoglobin was 5.4 (severe anemia) when she was brought into the hospital. She stated that mom had a fever of 102.6 and that she ordered a CT scan of her stomach and lungs. I interjected, asking, "How is my mom?" The doctor stated, "She passed away." I was in a state of shock and mortified as the physician told me that the CT scan of Mom's lungs was one of the worst she had ever seen in regard to COVID-19. The physician informed me that if she hadn't come to the hospital on Friday then she would have passed away at home. Furthermore, the coronavirus took advantage of my mother's weakened condition, namely her pre-existent lung disorder, chronic obstructive pulmonary disease (COPD), coupled with critically low hemoglobin, invariably weakened the immune system defenses and therefore played a significant role in her contracting this virus. Consequentially, the physician stated that my mother's lungs were overwhelmed by the coronavirus, therefore, they wouldn't have tolerated the support of the ventilator.

Tragically, Mom suffered a cardiac arrest early Sunday morning, March 29. I was informed that the medical personnel worked relentlessly for ten minutes to resuscitate her. Although the medical attempt failed, it was God's appointed time at 2:31 a.m. for my mother to step into eternity. No more pain for this tender-hearted matriarchal warrior! Finally, several minutes after learning about my mother's death, I cried aloud on the telephone, and the physician's voice seemed shaky as she too exhibited an emotional reaction. I was informed that the hospital had called my mother's telephone number at her apartment and that they called my cell number in Texas. I learned that the cell number prefixes were inadvertently transposed and this was the reason why I had never received a call from the hospital. After my conversation with the physician, I hung up the phone and felt like I was hit by a bolt of lightning. The news of my mother's death hit me like a freight train, causing me to sob uncontrollably in the arms of my wife, Valerie.

THE TSUNAMI ROLLERCOASTER

As the adrenaline kicked into high gear, I worked feverishly the following day to handle and close the affairs of my mother. After two and a half hours on the phone with the Social Security office, I immediately located a funeral home in Queens, New York, to arrange for Mom to be cremated. After faxing the paperwork and making a payment over the telephone, the funeral director stated that my mother was taken to the crematorium and had been cremated. After the phone call, I sobbed uncontrollably, and then regained my composure. My wife, Valerie, came inside to check on me. When I heard the word "crematorium" it was deeply disturbing to my soul. This coronavirus was like the Nazis, for the former took the lives of people around the world, while the latter utilized crematoriums to murder my people, the Jewish people. This was a chilling association, one that resided below the periphery of consciousness.

When the adrenaline dissipated, I felt a painful hole in my heart, a deep sadness that produced episodic moments of uncontrollable crying, followed by moments of calm. I recall deep sadness, while the inner pain was like the waves of a tsunami erupting with sheer intensity, then in a few minutes these emotional tidal waves seemed to dissipate to calm, serene water. I recall a few instances of walking, when suddenly my two legs lost strength and almost fell to the ground. The Dallas County shelter-in-place ordinance enabled me to cry aloud at home. I recall crying and opening my mouth, screaming silently within the depths of my soul. These emotional tsunami rollercoaster sensations would come and go as I tried to cope with the death of my mother. I remember as a kid riding the rollercoaster at the amusement park. After reaching the top, the downward plunge produced a frenzied rush to my senses. The difference with the actual rollercoaster ride was that after it was over I felt dizzy and would quell the motion sickness with Dramamine, while this emotional tsunami rollercoaster left me physically and emotionally drained, followed by an indescribable inner peace from God.

DESIGNED TO HEAL

I experienced the essence of humanness and learned a poignant lesson, namely, that these times of sadness constituted the process of bereavement. The God-man, Jesus Christ, cried and grieved for others. For instance, when Jesus learned about the death of his friend Lazarus, he cried (see John 11:35). When God designed us, he created within each human being the ability to grieve, then to heal. And it is important to know that our human brains were designed to protect us when emotions become intense during bouts of grief. The latter represents an inner device which God implanted within each and every one of us, and if our emotional reaction is intensified by grief, this internal thermostat immediately shifts into protective mode, ensuring that the person remains safe during intense crying. I have learned that tangible things act as triggers, setting off numerous emotions. For example, oftentimes letters, cards, or even a personal note from a deceased loved one initiates an emotional reaction, thus activating this emotional tsunami rollercoaster. For example, hours after learning about my mother's passing, my wife,

Valerie, handed me two sealed envelopes that my mother had given to be opened upon her death. One of the envelopes contained three words that were written in blue ink: "Open immediately upon . . ." This letter contained instructions and concluded with a personal message for me and my brother, Todd. Mom wrote:

> I love you both, and you have been my biggest joy in life. I will always watch over you!! Please overseer of Todd— tell him how proud I always was of him, and that I really died the day he had his accident on 11/17/88.

GRIEF AND THE BRAIN INJURED

Every time I read my mother's message, I would sob uncontrollably, triggering those insurmountable tsunami waves of emotion. The person for whom it would be hardest to hear the news would be my severely head-injured brother, Todd. His funds were depleted for full-time care at home, and he was relocated to a nursing facility in order to receive proper care. I arranged for the administrator's assistant, the social worker, and medical personnel to be on hand at this facility when I called my brother to share about Mom's death. I was concerned about how my brother would take the news. Faced with uncertainty about the outcome of sharing this news with Todd, I scheduled a FaceTime call to the facility on Tuesday, March 31. During the FaceTime call, the staff wore N95 face masks and then they aimed the camera towards Todd. I said, "Todd, I want you to look at me and listen. Mom has passed away." I read him an excerpt from my mother's letter: "I love you both, and you have been my biggest joy in life. I will always watch over you!!" I told Todd that Mom stated that she was always proud of him. While reading the letter, my wife, Valerie, and I sobbed as we informed Todd about Mom's death. Nevertheless, I reinforced to him that we have each other. Finally, I asked my brother if he understood what I had said to him about Mom. With a low-pitched moan, he stated, "Yes." The last three years of progressive neurological decline became evident as I observed my brother's stale affect during the FaceTime session, namely, the absence of emotional response. The personnel at the nursing home facility said after the FaceTime call that they observed Todd nod his head, an indication that he understood the conversation about the death of our mother.

Todd and me at his home, where he received full-time care for the severe traumatic brain injury. He was eventually relocated to a nursing facility because his funds for care became depleted.

For thirty-two years, my mother and I demonstrated steadfast love, care, and commitment for Todd's severe traumatic brain injury.

THE FLYING BLESSING

I was cleaning up from breakfast before the telephone call with Todd at the nursing facility, when my wife, Valerie, looked out the backyard window and exclaimed, "Oh no!" I wondered if she was commenting on something related to our lawn or the backyard. She said, "Look, a red cardinal. It means that a loved one is watching over you." We cried together, while six words from my mother's letter, "I will always watch over you!!," touched the core of my soul. In this letter, Mom spoke her heart to me and my brother, Todd, and whenever I read that she would always watch over us, I immediately thought about the red cardinal that sat gracefully on top of the wood fence pole. I do not believe in nor endorse reincarnation. However, from a figurative standpoint, Mom's presence flew into my life and reminded me about the deep bond, that infinite depth between a mother and a son.

Throughout the grief process, I have experienced an outpouring of God's grace, notably, the prayers and concerns from family, friends, and ministry colleagues. For example, I recall sobbing uncontrollably in bed with the covers over my head. I didn't want to awaken my wife and thought that crying under the bedcover would muffle the sound. As these tsunami waves of emotion flooded my heart, it felt like a bolt of electricity radiating throughout my whole body. Shortly thereafter, I felt a nudge on my leg and realized that my wife had touched me. I grabbed the warmth of her hand and silently cried, "Thank you, Jesus, for loving me." It was in this moment that the Lord reached out to comfort me. It is worth repeating, there were moments of stillness before the Lord (see Ps 46:10) and I discerned my mother's voice communing with my soul. I could feel her presence and her words comforted my despairing heart. It became evident to me that my mother is a part of me and I am a part of her. With that said, a rabbi friend shared a profound truth with me, for he taught me to recognize that although my mother is deceased, her voice speaks.[2]

---

2. Telephone call from Gregg L. Grossman to Dr. Rabbi Juan Marcos Bejarano Gutierrez, March 29, 2020. This comment was referenced from a eulogy for Rabbi Byron L. Sherwin. See Frydman-Kohl, "Byron L. Sherwin: 'Voice Still Speaks.'"

SEEKING GLOBAL RESTORATION

In the aftermath of this global pandemic lie the remaining vestiges of economic, psychological, and societal upheaval on earth. In fact, each life lost to the coronavirus possessed their own story, so to speak, leaving behind an indelible imprint on the hearts of loved ones, friends, and coworkers in the global community. Sadly, people with much to offer this world became casualties to this deleterious viral scourge of mankind. Moreover, the devastation from this terrible virus has dramatically disrupted the lives of its victims and family members. You may have lost your mother, father, husband, wife, fiancée, son, daughter, grandfather, grandmother, uncle, aunt, sibling, cousin, neighbor, coworker, or friend to this dreadful virus. My precious mother became a casualty to this silent invader of COVID-19. It is worth repeating, she was in a high-risk category, namely, the elderly with underlying medical issues (the lung disease COPD, and gastrointestinal bleeding).

Finally, as the incubation period ran its course, some people's symptoms were mild to moderate, while others soon thereafter worsened. It became apparent that the virus unleashed an inflammatory yet harmful attack on the pulmonary system, rendering many to be intubated and placed on ventilators in an intensive care unit, while others suffered numerous medical complications, especially blood clots and strokes, to name two. Albeit this silent invader reminded the world that the coronavirus was indicative of a twenty-first-century, modern-day plague, the soul of a wounded humanity yearns for global restoration.

WORDS OF COMFORT

The inception of this book chronicled an experiential account of my survival from personal and family traumatic brain injury, while providing a spiritual caricature of my journey to faith in Christ as a Reform Jew. For the aftermath of my mother's death from COVID-19 and the profound grief that followed became the catalyst for this postscript, namely, a voice to a wounded humanity in need of hope and healing on this battlefield called life. Moreover, I give praise to the unsung heroes, especially the medical personnel, police officers, firefighters, and the first responders who courageously faced this public health crisis with limited personal protective equipment (PPE), faithfully living out their role of service to God, society, and mankind. Finally, this global pandemic of COVID-19 has taken lives, crippled the economy, and weakened the mental, emotional, and social condition of humanity. With that said, I would like to pray for you:

> Heavenly Father, we come now with heads bowed and hearts open before you. The reader may have experienced physical, economic, psychological, and social hardship, while others have experienced grief, such as the death of a loved one or a friend from COVID-19. The loss of life is a deep pain which lingers in the heart. Father, comfort those that are hurting, struggling, and grieving the loss of a loved one from COVID-19. Help them to recognize that they are not alone. Eternal Father, give them the strength to endure the difficult days that lie ahead. Lord, protect the medical personnel, civil authorities, and the first responders, while providing healing for the physically and emotionally injured from this global pandemic. He walks with the broken hearted, for Christ states, "Blessed *are* those who mourn, For they shall be comforted" (Matt 5:4). Lord, help the burdened and the grief-stricken to hearken to these words from the psalmist:
>
>> But You, O LORD, *are* a God full of
>> compassion, and gracious,
>> Longsuffering and abundant
>> in mercy and truth. (Ps 86:15)
>
> Father, walk with the reader during these difficult times of physical, financial, and emotional uncertainty. As they navigate through this valley of affliction, provide them with wisdom, understanding, hope, and healing from the global pandemic of COVID-19. Thank you for this petition before your throne of mercy. Help them on this journey called life and empower them to follow an unseen and unheard One. The prophet Moses declares, "And the

Lord, He *is* the One who goes before you. He will be with you, He will not leave you nor forsake you; do not fear nor be dismayed" (Deut 31:8). I ask these prayer requests in the name of the Redeemer, Jesus Christ. Amen.

FINAL LESSON IN ACTION

This catastrophic public health crisis teaches us to embrace not only our loved ones, but the sanctity of life. And it is moments like this in our existence which act as the impetus to re-examine our spiritual condition, while considering the depth of our relationship with God. Although grief is a painful and uncomfortable process, albeit a natural reaction to the passing of a loved one, this will last for a season, and not for the rest of your life. Rather, we are confident that the Lord heals broken hearts from within in and certainly, in his time. Although you miss the presence of your loved one or friend, the Jewish prophet Isaiah brings assurance to your heart. Remember, you never walk alone because the Lord's comfort stands close to your grief-stricken soul. Isaiah declares:

> "The Spirit of the Lord GOD *is* upon Me,
> Because the LORD has anointed Me
> To preach good tidings to the poor;
> He has sent Me to heal the *brokenhearted* [emphasis added],
> To proclaim liberty to the captives,
> And the opening of the prison to *those who are* bound;
> To proclaim the acceptable year of the LORD,
> And the day of vengeance of our God;
> To comfort all who mourn,
> To console those who mourn in Zion,
> To give them beauty for ashes,
> The oil of joy for mourning,
> The garment of praise for the spirit of heaviness;
> That they may be called trees of righteousness,
> The planting of the LORD, that He may be glorified." (Isa 61:1–3)

Grief is draining and the slow process of healing oftentimes discourages the mourner from moving forward. As you express and feel these painful emotions, first, I want to encourage you to work through this gut-wrenching process, while drawing close to the Lord through prayer, contemplation, and fellowship. Take time to rest and heal in order to strengthen your emotional, mental, and spiritual health. May the words of the apostle Paul strengthen your faith, encourage your soul, and provide hope during the aftermath of COVID-19. He writes, "Now may the God of hope fill you with all joy and peace in believing, that you may abound in hope by the power of the Holy Spirit" (Rom 15:13).

Second, let me encourage you to consider this helpful exercise for grieving. If your loved one or friend were sitting at a table across from you right now, what would they tell you about how to handle their death?[3] I challenge you to share this with your counselor, pastor, rabbi, spiritual advisor, or close friend. I answered the aforementioned grief recovery question and, frankly, I found that my responses played a vital role with recovery from the grief associated with my mother's passing. Finally, although you cannot see things while you are going through the grieving process, you can rest assured that you are growing spiritually and emotionally through this valley of sorrow. My former professor from Norwich University encapsulated a deeply profound truth, "The best growth is the most painful."[4] You can do this! This is your Time of Perseverance.

3. Electronic message from Dr. Lynn A. Reichert to Gregg L. Grossman, April 3, 2020.

4. This comment is from my memory and was written by a psychology professor as a comment in one of my papers.

In Loving Memory
Lelia "Lee" M. Grossman
August 1, 1935—March 29, 2020
You fought hard to the end!

Suggested Reading

Brown, Michael L. *Answering Jewish Objections to Jesus: Theological Objections.* Vol. 2. Grand Rapids: Baker, 2000.

Calhoun, Adele Ahlberg. *Spiritual Disciplines Handbook: Practices That Transform Us.* Rev. ed. Downers Grove, IL: InterVarsity, 2015.

Fredriksen, Paula. *When Christians Were Jews: The First Generation.* New Haven, CT: Yale University Press, 2018.

Glaser, Mitch. *Isaiah 53 Explained.* New York: Chosen People, 2010.

Harvey, Richard. *Mapping Messianic Jewish Theology: A Constructive Approach.* Colorado Springs, CO: Paternoster, 2009.

Lizorkin-Eyzenberg, Eli. *The Jewish Gospel of John: Discovering Jesus, King of All Israel.* Tel Mond: Israel Study Center, 2015.

Morgan, Christopher W., and Robert A. Peterson, eds. *Fallen: A Theology of Sin.* Wheaton, IL: Crossway, 2013.

Owen, John. *Sin and Temptation: The Challenge of Personal Godliness.* Edited by James M. Houston. Classics of Faith and Devotion. Minneapolis: Bethany House, 1996.

Rudolph, David, and Joel Willitts, eds. *Introduction to Messianic Judaism: Its Ecclesial Context and Biblical Foundations.* Grand Rapids: Zondervan, 2013.

Stern, David H. *Restoring the Jewishness of the Gospel: A Message for Christians.* (Condensed from Messianic Jewish Manifesto). 2nd ed. Clarksville, MD: Jewish New Testament, 1990.

About the Author

Gregg L. Grossman was born in New York City, New York, and was raised in Queens, which comprises one of the five boroughs of New York City. He graduated from Cheshire Academy and received a Bachelor of Science degree in communications, *summa cum laude*, from Norwich University. Moreover, he earned graduate credit in mental health counseling at Nova Southeastern University (formerly Nova University) and in Christian education at Dallas Theological Seminary. He has spent twenty-four successful years in sales and marketing. His sales career started in the research department for a television production company that specialized in paid programming for television shows that appeared on ABC, PBS, and CNBC. Gregg became a junior recruiter and pursued work in the recruiting and staffing industries for several years before transitioning into business-to-business corporate sales. He earned an MDiv degree in pastoral ministry (high distinction) and a PhD degree (high distinction) at Trinity Theological Seminary.

Presently, he works in the Dallas Division as a bivocational workplace chaplain for Marketplace Chaplains, and acts as the frontline staff to share God's love (John 3:16; Rom 5:8). Dr. Grossman teaches as an adjunct professor at Louisiana Baptist University and Seminary. He is the president of Beyond Perseverance LLC, a Christian life coaching company that helps people achieve sustainable life change in order to enhance their professional and personal lives. Gregg holds dual certifications as a Biblical Life Coach and a Life Breakthrough Coach from Life Breakthrough Academy.

His writing, speaking, and teaching exemplify a life dedicated toward serving others. Dr. Grossman remains passionate about living out a genuine life before the people, while mentoring, coaching, and discipling people to become the person God has called them to be in life.

Contact Information

Linkedin: https://www.linkedin.com/in/gregg-l-grossman-ph-d-55126119/
Website: http://www.beyondperseverance.com
Facebook Profile: https://www.facebook.com/profile.
php?id=100053475242255
Facebook Ministry Page: Times of Perseverance,
https://www.facebook.com/chesed28/
Email: gregg@beyondperseverance.com

I am available for speaking engagements. Please email your contact
information and the requested date and time to speak to:
speak@beyondperseverance.com.

All other contact and inquiries: info@beyondperseverance.com

Bibliography

Barclay, William. *The Gospel of John*. Vol. 1. The Daily Study Bible. Philadelphia: Westminster, 1956.

Calhoun, Adele Ahlberg. *Spiritual Disciplines Handbook: Practices That Transform Us*. Downers Grove, IL: InterVarsity, 2005.

Elliott, Elbert E. "Evangelistic Preaching." Webinar, Trinity College of the Bible and Theological Seminary, June 12, 2014.

Frydman-Kohl, Baruch. "Byron L. Sherwin: 'The Voice Still Speaks.'" *Journal of Jewish Ethics* 2.1 (2016) 112–19.

Glidewell, Charles. "From Desperation to Faith." Lesson 10 in *Miracles: The Transforming Power of Jesus (A Study of Matthew)*, by Julie (Brown) Wood, Vivian Conrad, Charles Glidewell, and John Beck, 93–100. Connect 360 Bible Study Guide. Dallas: BaptistWay, 2019.

Golding, Bruce. "Roadside Surgery May Have Saved Life." *Gannett Westchester Newspapers*, November 19, 1988, Community, A3.

Graham, Billy. *Hope for the Troubled Heart*. Minneapolis: Grason, 1991.

Grossman, Gregg. "Honduran President Visits Campus, Praises NU Participation in Partnership Program." *The Guidon* 72.14 (April 26, 1990). Norwich University.

Hagin, Kenneth E. *God's Medicine*. Faith Library Cassette Series 63H. Kenneth Hagin Ministries, 1992.

———. "My Testimony of Healing." Message recorded on cassette tape. In *God's Medicine*. Faith Library Cassette Series 63H. Kenneth Hagin Ministries, 1992.

Hagin, Kenneth, Jr. "Getting to Know Your Teacher." Message recorded on cassette tape. In *Rhema Favorites*, Faith Library Cassette Series 18J. Kenneth Hagin Ministries, 1988.

———. *Rhema Favorites*. Faith Library Cassette Series 18J. Kenneth Hagin Ministries, 1988.

Hughes, R. Kent. *Disciplines of a Godly Man*. 10th anniversary edition, revised. Wheaton, IL: Crossway, 2001.

Kennedy, D. James. *Evangelism Explosion: Equipping Churches for Friendship, Evangelism, Discipleship, and Healthy Growth*. 4th ed. Wheaton, IL: Tyndale, 1996.

Norwich University convocation program, Sept. 4th, 1990. Commencement Ephemera Collection, 1990 file, Norwich University Archives, Kreitzberg Library, Northfield, VT.

Parrett Gary A. and S. Steve Kang. *Teaching the Faith, Forming the Faithful: A Biblical Vision for Education in the Church*. Downers Grove, IL: InterVarsity, 2009.

Rudolph, David. "Introduction." In *Introduction to Messianic Judaism: Its Ecclesial Context and Biblical Foundations*, edited by David Rudolph and Joel Willitts, 11–18. Grand Rapids: Zondervan, 2013.

Schreiber, Mordecai, Alvin I. Schiff, and Leon Klenicki, eds. *The Shengold Jewish Encyclopedia*. Rockville, MD: Shengold, 1998.

Sunnyvale First Baptist Church. *Order of Worship*, April 22, 2012.

Swindoll, Charles R. *Growing Strong in the Seasons of Life*. Grand Rapids: Zondervan, 1983.

———. "When God Says 'No.'" *Kindred Spirit* 21/3 (Autumn 1997) 6–7.

Wiersbe, Warren W. *The Bible Exposition Commentary: New Testament*. Vol. 2, *Ephesians–Revelation*. Colorado Springs, CO: David C. Cook, 1989.

Wiesel, Elie, *Night*. Translated by Marion Wiesel. New York: Hill and Wang, 2006.

Willard, Dallas. *Renovation of the Heart: Putting on the Character of Christ*. Colorado Springs, CO: NavPress, 2002.

Made in the USA
Coppell, TX
28 September 2021